Advanced
Wiring
PRO TIPS AND SIMPLE STEPS

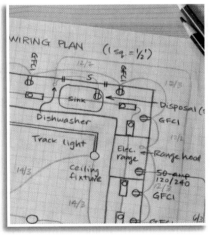

Meredith® Books
Des Moines, Iowa

Stanley® Books
An imprint of Meredith® Books

Stanley Advanced Wiring
Editor: Ken Sidey
Senior Associate Design Director: Tom Wegner
Assistant Editor: Harijs Priekulis
Copy Chief: Terri Fredrickson
Editorial Operations Manager: Karen Schirm
Managers, Book Production: Pam Kvitne,
    Marjorie J. Schenkelberg
Technical Editors, The Stanley Works: Mike Maznio,
    Jim Olsen
Contributing Copy Editor: Jim Stepp
Technical Proofreader: Ralph Selzer
Contributing Proofreaders: Sue Fetters, Ray Kast,
    Debra Morris Smith
Electronic Production Coordinator: Paula Forest
Editorial and Design Assistants: Kathleen Stevens

Additional Editorial Contributions from
    Greenleaf Publishing
Publishing Director: Dave Toht
Writer: Steve Cory
Editorial Art Director: Jean DeVaty
Design: Rebecca Anderson
Editorial Assistant: Betony Toht
Photography: Dan Stultz, Stultz Photography
Illustrator: Dave Brandon, Art Rep Services
Technical Consultant: Joe Hansa
Indexer: Nan Badgett

Meredith® Books
Editor in Chief: James D. Blume
Design Director: Matt Strelecki
Managing Editor: Gregory H. Kayko
Executive Editor, Gardening and Home Improvement:
    Benjamin W. Allen
Executive Editor, Home Improvement: Larry Erickson

Director, Sales, Special Markets: Rita McMullen
Director, Sales, Premiums: Michael A. Peterson
Director, Sales, Retail: Tom Wierzbicki
Director, Book Marketing: Brad Elmitt
Director, Operations: George A. Susral
Director, Production: Douglas M. Johnston

Meredith Publishing Group
President, Publishing Group: Stephen M. Lacy

Meredith Corporation
Chairman and Chief Executive Officer: William T. Kerr
Chairman of the Executive Committee: E.T. Meredith III

All of us at Stanley® Books are dedicated to providing you with the information and ideas you need to enhance your home and garden. We welcome your comments and suggestions about this book. Write to us at:
    Meredith Corporation
    Stanley Books
    1716 Locust St.
    Des Moines, IA 50309–3023

If you would like more information on other Stanley products, call 1-800-STANLEY or visit us at: www.stanleyworks.com Stanley® and the notched rectangle around the Stanley name are registered trademarks of The Stanley Works and subsidiaries.

If you would like to purchase any of our home improvement, cooking, crafts, gardening, or home decorating and design books, check wherever quality books are sold. Or visit us at: meredithbooks.com

Note to the Readers: Due to differing conditions, tools, and individual skills, Meredith Corporation assumes no responsibility for any damages, injuries suffered, or losses incurred as a result of following the information published in this book. Before beginning any project, review the instructions carefully, and if any doubts or questions remain, consult local experts or authorities. Because codes and regulations vary greatly, you always should check with authorities to ensure that your project complies with all applicable local codes and regulations. Always read and observe all of the safety precautions provided by manufacturers of any tools, equipment, or supplies, and follow all accepted safety procedures.

CONTENTS

ASSEMBLING
TOOLS &
MATERIALS

Though many homeowners fear working with electricity, wiring is an amateur-friendly trade. A handy person carefully following instructions can produce safe and reliable electrical installations. Attention to detail is the key.

Are you ready for this book?
This book presents projects that require running new cable. To learn about simpler projects—repairs, replacing devices, and replacing fixtures—see *Stanley Basic Wiring*. In that book you will also find an introduction to household wiring, as well as tips on inspecting your system for problems.

Before you begin a project in this book,

understand how to shut off power and know how to test that power is off *(pages 6–7)*. Know how to strip wires, splice wires together, and join wires to terminals. These skills are simple but essential for safe, secure, and reliable electrical connections.

This first chapter describes the tools and supplies needed for electrical projects. Planning New Electrical Service guides you through important preliminary steps that prevent frustrations and problems later on. It also explains how to work with a local building department to ensure your project meets electrical safety code.

Hands-on work begins with Installing

Cables and Boxes. The second half of the book gets into specific projects: Installing Lights and Outlets, Vent Fans, and Outdoor Wiring. The final chapter, Completing New Circuits, deals with connections in the service panel, as well as how to wire appliances.

How to use this book
Each project includes a Prestart Checklist, which outlines the time, skills, tools, materials, and preparations needed. In addition to the project steps, you'll find Stanley Pro Tips and other extra information. Since no two houses are exactly alike, "What If..." boxes provide help for unusual situations.

Proper tools and quality materials save time and help ensure a safe and reliable installation.

CHAPTER PREVIEW

Working safely
page 6

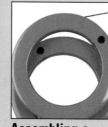
Assembling a tool kit
page 8

Special-duty tools
page 10

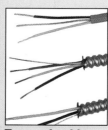
Types of cable
page 11

Check the instructions or packaging of the fixtures you plan to install for wattage and any special installation requirements.

Your local building department has guidelines that describe what permits and inspections are required for electrical projects.

To learn how to draw up a plan suitable for applying for a permit, *see pages 28–29.*

Electrical boxes
page 12

Fasteners and clamps
page 14

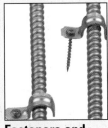

Wire nuts
page 15

You don't need an elaborate computer design program or a drafting table to work out plans for an electrical project. A pad of graph paper, a ruler, and some colored pencils will do the job. In addition to this book, you will need information on safety code requirements from your local building department.

WORKING SAFELY

Approach household electricity with caution and respect. Professional electricians take steps to ensure themselves double and even triple protection against shocks. You need to be just as careful. To stay safe while doing the work, learn these precautions and turn them into work habits.

Be insulated

The effect of a shock varies according to how much power is present, your physical constitution, and how well insulated you are. Don't wear loose-fitting clothing that can get tangled in wires. Wear rubber-soled shoes. Remove jewelry. Keep yourself dry. If the floor of your work area is damp or wet, put down some dry boards and stand on them. Use rubber-gripped tools.

If you are wearing dry clothes and rubber-soled shoes, receiving a 120-volt shock will grab your attention, but it probably will not harm you. However, if you have a heart condition or are particularly sensitive to shock, the effects could be more serious. If you haven't taken proper precautions, chances are greater that a shock could cause injury. If you are working with 240-volt current, the danger is much greater.

Shut off the power

Before starting any electrical project, always shut off power to the circuit. Then test to make sure there is no power present in the electrical box or wires.

You may be tempted to skip this step and save a trip to the service panel. Or you may think you can change a receptacle or light without touching any wires, but don't take that risk. It takes only a few minutes to provide yourself with the necessary protection against shock.

Pretend it's live

Professional electricians have this simple rule: **Even after shutting off power, always act as if the wires are live.** That way, if someone accidentally turns on the power, or a tester gives the wrong reading, you're still protected.

One final tip: Eliminate all distractions when working on wiring. Banish family members—especially children—from the area. Turn off the radio, and let the answering machine pick up phone calls.

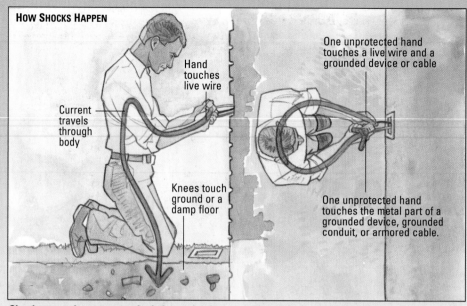

HOW SHOCKS HAPPEN

Hand touches live wire

Current travels through body

Knees touch ground or a damp floor

One unprotected hand touches a live wire and a grounded device or cable

One unprotected hand touches the metal part of a grounded device, grounded conduit, or armored cable.

Shocks occur because your body is conductive and can become a path for electricity. Here's how shocks happen:

You become the pathway to ground. If you touch only a hot wire (usually black or colored), current passes through you and toward the ground. To greatly reduce or eliminate a shock, wear rubber-soled shoes and/or stand on a thick, nonconducting surface (such as a dry wood floor).

You become part of the circuit. If you touch both a hot (black or colored) wire and a neutral (white) wire or a ground (green or bare copper) wire at the same time, your body completes the circuit and current passes through you. If this happens, you can receive a painful shock even when standing on a nonconductive surface. Avoid touching any bare wire; use rubber-gripped tools and hold them only by the handle.

SAFETY ALERT
Safety glasses and rubber-gripped tools

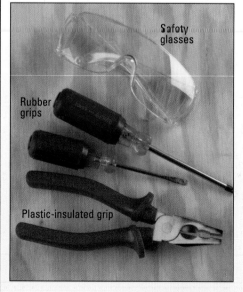

Safety glasses

Rubber grips

Plastic-insulated grip

Electrician's tools have heavy-duty rubber grips to protect hands from wayward power. Use these special tools *(pages 8–9)* rather than regular carpentry tools. Always grasp them by the rubber grips—never touch the metal parts of the tools.

Safety glasses are a good idea when you're doing any construction work. They protect your eyes from irritants such as drywall or plaster dust, which flies up whenever holes are being cut in walls or ceilings. More importantly, safety glasses guard your eyes against dangerous bits of metal that can fly when you saw metal or snip wires. Porcelain and glass fixtures also can chip and pose hazards.

Checking that power is off

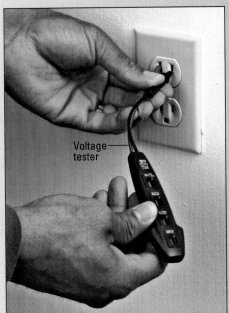

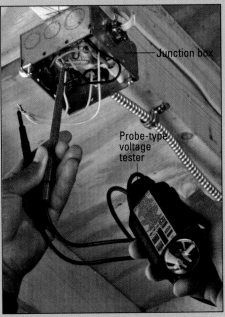

Circuit index shows which outlets each breaker or fuse controls

Voltage tester

Junction box

Probe-type voltage tester

1 At the service panel, flip off the breaker or unscrew the fuse controlling the electrical box or device you will work on.

2 Test for the presence of power using a voltage tester. If you are working on a receptacle, test both plugs. Test the tester, too. Touch the probes to a live circuit to make sure the indicator bulb lights.

3 It's possible that a single box has more than one circuit running through it. Carefully remove the device or fixture, unscrew the wire nuts, and test all the wires for power.

REFRESHER COURSE: Testing tools

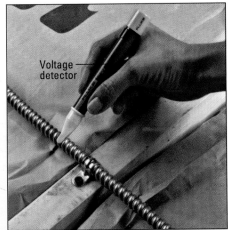

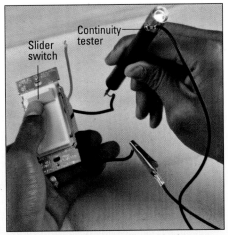

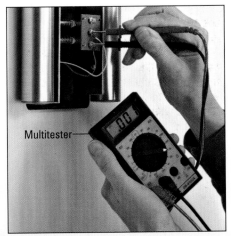

Voltage detector

Slider switch

Continuity tester

Multitester

A voltage detector senses the presence of power inside cables and, in some cases, even inside walls. Before using it, test this battery-powered tool on a line you know to be live. If the end glows, the tester is working.

A continuity tester determines whether a break in wiring or electrical contacts exists. Use it to test a fuse, a switch, or the wiring in a lamp or light fixture. Use it only when the power is off.

A multitester does the work of both a voltage tester and a continuity tester. Use it also to test low-voltage wiring, such as in a door chime or appliance. A digital model is easier to use than one with a needle.

ASSEMBLING A TOOL KIT

Don't skimp when buying tools for electrical work; your safety and the quality of the installation are at stake. Assembling a complete kit of professional-quality electricians' tools will cost far less than hiring a professional to do even a simple installation.

Wiring tools
These tools enable you to cut, strip, and join wires tightly. A pair of **side cutters** (also called diagonal cutters) makes working inside a crowded electrical box or snipping off sheathing from nonmetallic cable easier.

Cutting pliers help with general chores such as snipping armored cable. Use **longnose pliers** to bend wires into loops before attaching them to terminals. The **combination strippers** shown below—with holes for the wires near the tip—are easier to use than strippers with holes back near the handle. Use **lineman's pliers** to twist wires together after stripping them; no other tool works as well. You can also use lineman's pliers to cut wire.

Use **screwdrivers** designed especially for electrical use. They have thick rubber grips, which shield a hand from shock. You'll most often use screwdrivers with 6- to 7-inch shanks; buy two sizes of slot screwdrivers and two sizes of phillips screwdrivers. Occasionally you may need a short "stubby." A **wire-bending screwdriver** quickly forms a perfect loop in a stripped wire end. A **rotary screwdriver** drives screws quickly; use it when you have several coverplates to install.

Testers
For most work, you will need a **voltage tester** to test for the presence of power, and a **continuity tester** to see whether a device

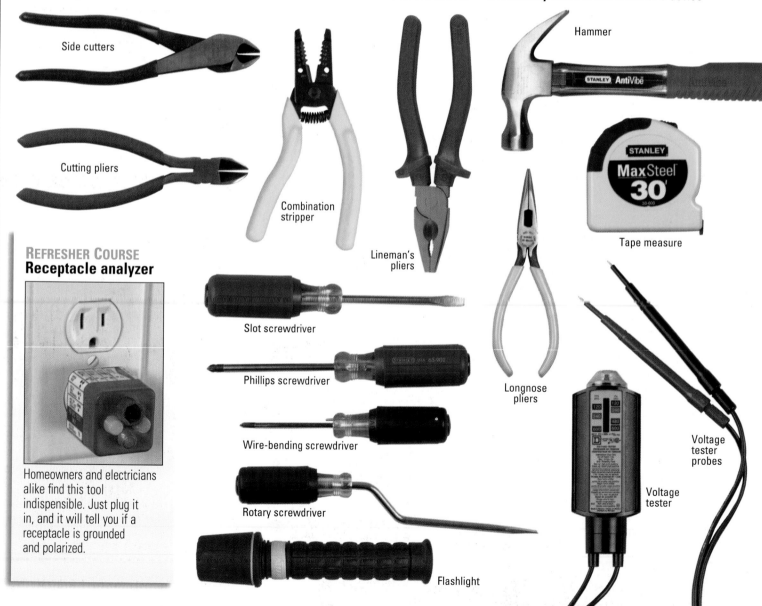

Side cutters

Cutting pliers

Combination stripper

Lineman's pliers

Hammer

Tape measure

Longnose pliers

Slot screwdriver

Phillips screwdriver

Wire-bending screwdriver

Rotary screwdriver

Flashlight

Voltage tester probes

Voltage tester

REFRESHER COURSE
Receptacle analyzer

Homeowners and electricians alike find this tool indispensible. Just plug it in, and it will tell you if a receptacle is grounded and polarized.

or fixture is damaged inside. A **multitester** does the job of both but is a bit more complicated to use. Professional-quality testers have probes and clips with thick rubber grips and lights or readouts that are clearly visible.

In addition, you may want a **voltage detector,** which senses power through cable sheathing, a box cover, or even a wall or ceiling. (Testers are shown in use on *page 7.*) Also buy a **receptacle analyzer** *(page 8).*

General tools
For jobs that involve running cable, assemble a tool bucket's worth of carpentry hand tools. Keep a reliable **flashlight** within easy reach, in case you have to work with the lights off. A **hammer** and a pair of **channel-lock pliers** come in handy for just about any wiring job. To remove moldings with minimal damage, use a **pry bar.** Make initial cuts in walls and ceilings with a **utility knife.** Complete the cuts in plaster walls with a **saber saw;** use a **drywall saw** to cut through drywall. Use a **hacksaw** to cut rigid conduit and to cut through screws holding boxes.

Fishing tools
These tools help minimize damage to walls and ceilings when running cable. A ⅜-**inch drill** is powerful enough for most household projects; rent or buy a ½-inch model for extensive work. In addition to a standard ¾-**inch spade bit,** buy a **fishing bit,** which can reach across two studs or joists and pull cable back through the holes it has made *(page 52).*

You can use a straightened coat hanger wire to fish cable through short runs, but a **fish tape** is easier to use *(pages 52–53).* Occasionally you may need to run one tape from each direction so buy two. Also use a fish tape when pulling wires through conduit *(page 41).*

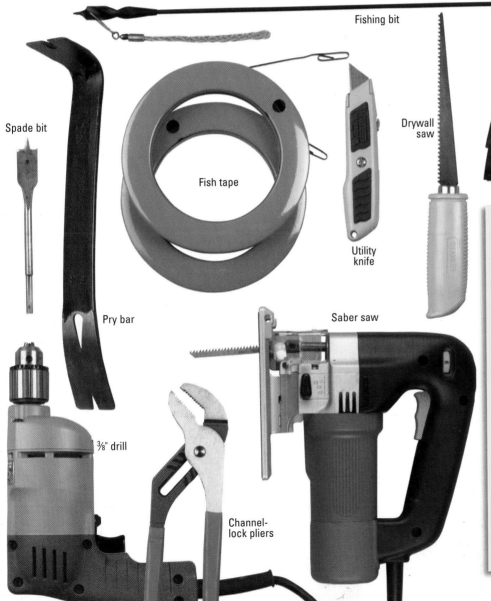

Fishing bit

Spade bit

Hacksaw

Drywall saw

Fish tape

Utility knife

Pry bar

Saber saw

⅜" drill

Channel-lock pliers

STANLEY PRO TIP

Electrician's tool belt

An electrician's tool belt holds all the tools you need and it will help you keep electrician's tools separate from general tools.

SPECIAL-DUTY TOOLS

The tools shown on *pages 8–9* are needed for almost any wiring project. They're essential for any wiring project that involves running new lines. The tools on this page are specialized. Buy or rent them only as the need arises.

Cutting tools

If you have old plaster walls, cutting into them to run cable is difficult and messy. There's no simple solution, but many people find that it helps to use a **rotary-cutting tool**. It slices through both the lath and plaster without vibrating. It does, however, kick up a good deal of dust.

A **reciprocating saw** cuts notches in walls quickly and is ideal for reaching into tight spots. Use this tool carefully if you suspect electrical cable may lie behind the wall or ceiling surface; if in doubt, use a hand saw.

When running outdoor electrical lines *(pages 104–105)*, a simple **spade** is usually all you need. Rent a trencher for projects requiring a lot of digging. Use a **clamshell digger** to dig postholes.

Tools for drilling holes

A ⅜-inch drill is powerful enough to drill six or seven holes in an hour, but it will overheat and even break if you use it continuously. If you have a lot of drilling to do, rent or buy a heavy-duty ½-**inch drill**. The right-angle model shown below makes it possible to drill straight holes in studs and joists. For leveling and plumbing boxes, use a **torpedo level**. To make sure your holes are level with each other, use a 4-foot or 8-foot **carpenter's level**.

Other useful tools

Most electrical components are fastened with screws, but some use nuts. For these, use a **nut driver** or a socket and ratchet. A **conduit reamer** slips onto a square-shanked screwdriver to clean out pieces of metal conduit cut by a hacksaw. A **cordless screwdriver** saves time if you are installing many devices. Often framing will need notching and trimming—have a ¾-inch **wood chisel** on hand.

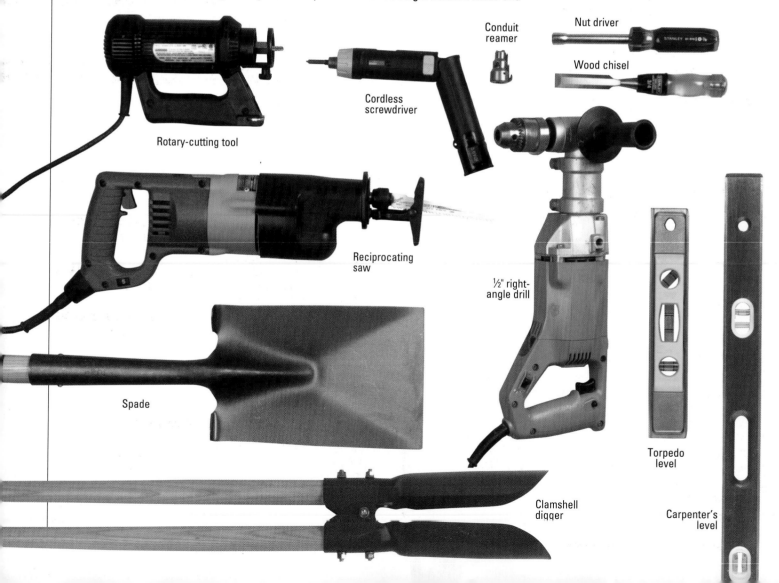

Rotary-cutting tool

Cordless screwdriver

Conduit reamer

Nut driver

Wood chisel

Reciprocating saw

½" right-angle drill

Spade

Torpedo level

Clamshell digger

Carpenter's level

TYPES OF CABLE

Make sure that the cable being installed will handle the electrical load safely and satisfy building code requirements *(page 23)*. Cable packaging indicates the gauge and number of wires. For example, "12/2" means two (black and white) 12-gauge wires, plus a ground wire.

Nonmetallic (NM) cable, sometimes called Romex, has two or three insulated wires, plus a bare ground wire, wrapped in plastic sheathing *(pages 34–35)*. Many local codes permit NM cable inside walls or ceilings, and some codes allow it to be exposed in basements and garages. **Underground feeder (UF) cable** has wires wrapped in solid plastic for watertight protection. Use it for outdoor projects *(pages 104–105)*.

Armored cable encases insulated wires in metal sheathing for added protection. **Metal-clad (MC)** has a green-insulated ground wire. **BX (also called AC)** has no ground wire, only a thin aluminum wire unsuitable as a ground; the metal sheathing provides the path for grounding. Some local codes require armored cable or conduit *(see below)* wherever wiring is exposed.

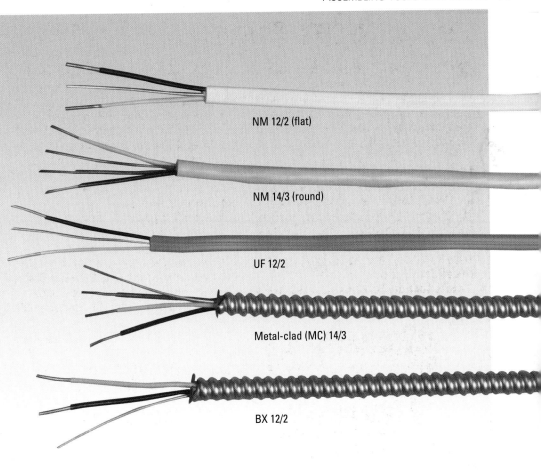

NM 12/2 (flat)

NM 14/3 (round)

UF 12/2

Metal-clad (MC) 14/3

BX 12/2

Conduit types

EMT rigid metal conduit

PVC ½" conduit

Greenfield

EMT ½"

Conduit—pipe that wires run through—offers the best protection against damage to wires. It also makes it easy to change or install new wires in the future: Pull the wires through the conduit, rather than cutting into walls to run new cable.

Metal conduit *(pages 38–39)* once was used as a path for grounding; recent codes require a green-insulated ground wire. **PVC (plastic) conduit** is cheaper but not quite as strong *(page 40)*. Metal **Greenfield** and plastic **EMT tubing** are flexible types of conduit. They are expensive but useful when working in tight spots.

Wire colors and sizes

The thicker a wire, the more amperage (amps) it can carry without overheating. A #14 wire carries up to 15 amps; a #12 wire, up to 20 amps; and a #10 wire, up to 30 amps. Never overload a wire—for instance, never place a #14 wire on a 20-amp circuit.

Wires coated with insulation that is black, red, or another color are hot wires, carrying power out from the service panel to the electrical user. (White wires are neutral, meaning they carry power back to the service panel.) Green or bare wires are ground wires. **Be aware, however, that not all electrical work has been done correctly, so the wires in your house could be the wrong color.**

HOT WIRES

#14 red

#12 blue

#10 brown

#12 black

GROUND WIRES

#12 green

#12 copper

ELECTRICAL BOXES

Wiring installations usually begin by adding a box. All connections—whether splices or connections to terminals—must be made inside a code-approved electrical box. (Some fixtures, such as fluorescent and recessed lights, have self-contained electrical boxes approved by most building departments.)

Plastic or metal?

Check with your building department to see whether plastic boxes are acceptable. Some municipalities require metal boxes, which are more expensive but usually no more trouble to install. Use special boxes for outdoor work *(page 102)*.

In older systems that use conduit or the sheathing of armored cable as a grounding path, the boxes must be metal because they are part of the grounding system *(page 22)*. Homes with NM or MC cable use green-insulated or bare copper wires for grounding and don't require metal boxes. However, some local codes call for metal boxes, which provide a stronger bond for the grounding wire *(page 22)*.

Remodel and new-work boxes

A remodel box has fittings that secure it to a finished wall. Plastic boxes have "wings" *(page 13, far right)*; metal boxes have expandable clips or bendable ears that hold them in the wall *(page 49)*. See *pages 48–49* for various types and how to install them. Remodel boxes all have internal clamps that clasp the cable to the box.

New-work boxes install quickly in framing that has not been covered with drywall or plaster *(page 44)*. To install most models, hold the box in place (allowing the box to

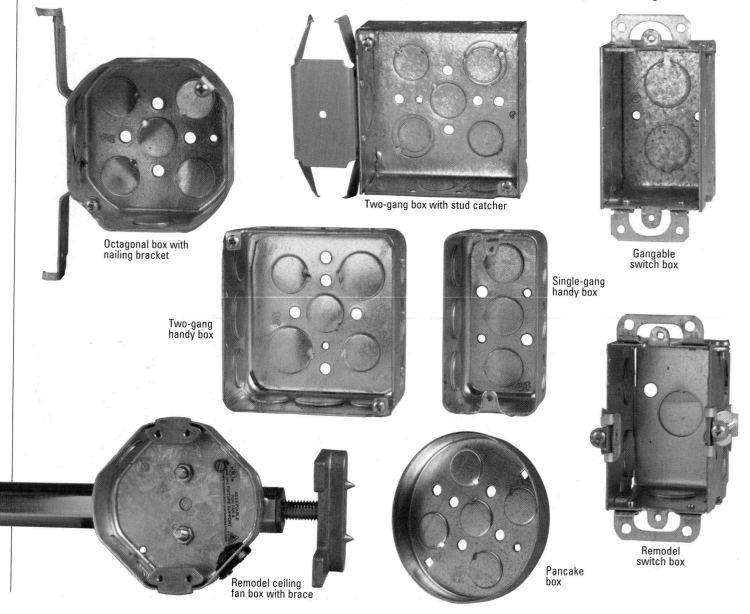

Two-gang box with stud catcher

Octagonal box with nailing bracket

Gangable switch box

Two-gang handy box

Single-gang handy box

Remodel ceiling fan box with brace

Pancake box

Remodel switch box

protrude beyond the framing far enough to allow for the thickness of the wall material) and drive two nails.

Number of gangs

A "single-gang" box has room and screw holes for one switch or receptacle; a "two-gang" box has room for two, and so on. "Gangable" metal boxes can be partly dismantled and joined together to form a box of as many gangs as are needed.

Adapter rings

A box may be installed with its front edge flush with the wall or ceiling. Or the box may be installed ½ inch behind the wall, in which case an adapter ring, also called a "mud ring," is installed onto the front edge of the box. Use a 4×4-inch box and a single-gang mud ring when installing a 240-volt receptacle *(page 60-61)* so there will be room for the wiring.

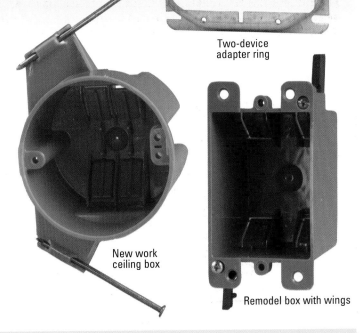

Two-device adapter ring

Single-gang box

Ceiling remodel box

New work ceiling box

Remodel box with wings

Two-gang box

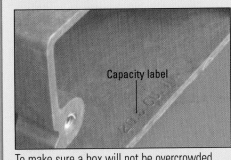

STANLEY PRO TIP: **Boxes that are big enough**

Capacity label

To make sure a box will not be overcrowded, always buy as big a box as will fit the space available. The cubic-inch capacity of electrical boxes should be listed by the store selling them. To calculate whether a box will be crowded, use these figures: A #14 wire takes up 2 cubic inches; a #12 wire takes up 2.25 cubic inches. Count the fixture or device as one wire. For instance, this box contains eight #12 "wires"—two blacks, two whites, three grounds, and one receptacle—for a total of 18 cubic inches.

FASTENERS AND CLAMPS

In addition to cable and boxes, electrical jobs call for a few other supplies: tape, staples, or straps to secure cable to framing members, and clamps that hold cable to boxes.

Light fixtures usually come with all the necessary hardware for fastening to the ceiling box. If you have old boxes, you may need to buy extra hardware.

Cable fasteners

Codes require that all exposed cable be tightly stapled to the wall, ceiling, or a framing member. Also use staples when running cable in unfinished framing. For NM cable, buy plastic-insulated staples that are the right size for the cable.

To anchor metal conduit, hammer in drive straps every few feet. For PVC conduit or armored cable, use one- or two-hole straps; make sure they fit snugly around the cable or conduit.

Avoid the black drywall (or all-purpose) screws because they break easily. Wood screws cost more but are more reliable.

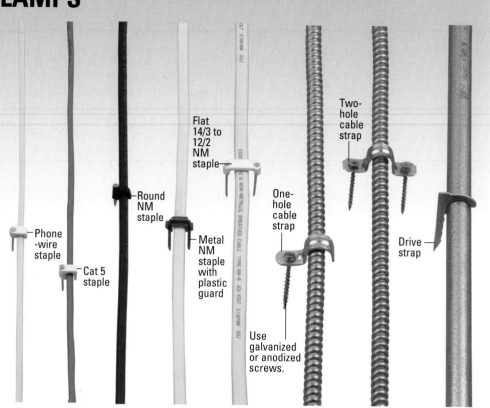

Phone-wire staple

Cat 5 staple

Round NM staple

Metal NM staple with plastic guard

Flat 14/3 to 12/2 NM staple

One-hole cable strap

Use galvanized or anodized screws.

Two-hole cable strap

Drive strap

Clamp types

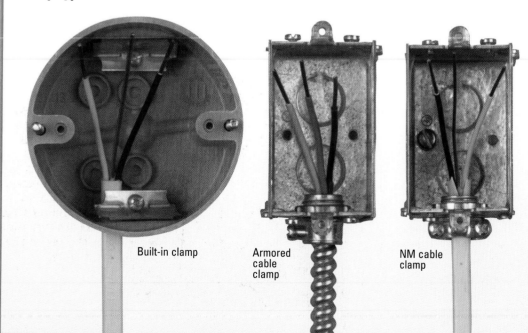

Built-in clamp

Armored cable clamp

NM cable clamp

New-work plastic boxes have holes with plastic flaps that lightly grab NM cable. With that type of box, you must staple the cable to a framing member near the box (page 35). Use these only in unfinished framing. When installing a remodel box or when installing a box that will be exposed, the cable or conduit must be firmly clamped directly to the box.

A cable clamp comes in two parts: the clamp and the lock nut. An NM clamp holds the cable using a strap with two screws; an armored-cable clamp holds the cable using a single setscrew.

For instructions on how to clamp cable to a box, see page 35.

WIRE NUTS

In old installations, wire splices often were covered with thick electrician's tape. That is not only a slow way to cover a splice, but it is also a code violation. Cover every splice with an approved wire nut.

Assemble a collection of various size nuts so you will be ready for any splice. Wire nuts are color-coded according to size. The colors and sizes may vary according to manufacturer; read the containers to make sure the nuts you buy will fit over your splices. The most common arrangement is like this:

■ The smallest wire nuts—which usually come with a light fixture—are often white, ivory, or blue. If these have plastic rather than metal threads inside, throw them away and get orange connectors with metal threads for a secure connection.
■ Orange nuts are the next size up and can handle splices of up to two #14 wires.
■ Midsize yellow wire nuts are the most common. Use them for splices as small as two #14s or as large as three #12s.
■ Red connectors are usually the largest

wire nuts and can handle a splice of up to four #12s.
■ Green wire nuts are used for ground wires. They have a hole in the top, which allows one ground wire to poke through and run directly to a device or box.
■ Gray "twister" wire nuts are designed to be all-purpose—they can handle the smallest to the largest splices. However, they are also bulky and expensive.
■ "B-cap" wire nuts are slim, which makes them useful if a box is crowded with wires.

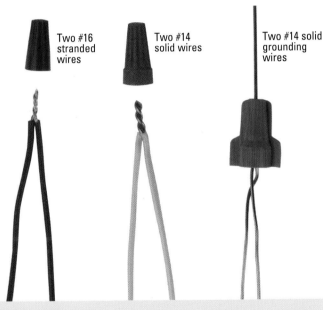

Two #16 stranded wires

Two #14 solid wires

Two #14 solid grounding wires

Three #12 wires

Four #12 wires

All-purpose "twister" wire nuts

Space-saving B-cap wire nuts

STANLEY PRO TIP: **Good tape**

Professional-quality electrician's tape costs more than bargain-bin tape, but it sticks better and is easier to work with.

You should cut pieces of tape rather than ripping them off the roll; ripped pieces have rippled ends that do not stick. Cutting with a utility knife is often awkward and time-consuming, so buy tape in a dispenser—just pull out and down to make a clean cut.

REFRESHER COURSE
Grounding pigtail

Grounding screw

Grounding pigtail

If codes require you to attach grounds to metal boxes, save time and work by buying grounding pigtails. If your boxes do not already have them, buy green-tinted grounding screws that fit into threaded holes in the boxes.

Planning New Electrical Service

Anytime you install new electrical cable—adding just one receptacle or installing wiring for a remodeled kitchen—you are adding new service to your system. Because you may be increasing the demand on circuits or adding entire circuits, new service calls for careful planning.

Put your plans on paper

The first step is to make rough drawings that depict the lighting and electrical service you want to achieve. *Pages 18–21* show typical electrical systems for a kitchen, a bathroom, and utility rooms. Your installations will vary; these pages serve as a guide to help calculate how many circuits of which amperages are needed. Start planning cable runs that can be routed to do minimal damage to walls.

Next, figure out whether your existing service can support new electrical lines. You may be able simply to connect to existing circuits. Or you may need to add a circuit or two to your existing service panel or install a subpanel or a new service panel. *Pages 26–27* guide you through those calculations.

Why codes count

The importance of building safety codes can't be overemphasized. First, codes protect you and everyone in your home from shock and fire. Second, they provide common ground for everyone who works on electrical systems. When someone else works on your home's wiring after you, he or she will be able to understand the system.

Check local codes

Pages 22–23 describe requirements throughout much of the country. However, codes can vary from town to town, so contact your local building department when planning a project. Have your rough drawings and finished plans reviewed by the department. See *pages 28–29* for tips on drawing plans that an inspector will be able to read easily. Follow the department's instructions and schedule inspections if needed. Do no work until you are sure it will be approved.

Adding new service calls for carefully assessing demand and making detailed project plans.

Chapter Preview

Wiring a kitchen
page 18

Wiring a bathroom
page 20

Wiring utility rooms
page 21

Codes often encountered
page 22

Jobs that involve running new cable typically require a permit.

Post your work permit in a highly visible location.

Once you have presented acceptable plans to your building department, you will receive a work permit. Follow the inspection schedule and instructions to the letter.

Loading circuits for safety
page 24

Checking out your basic service
page 26

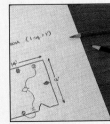

Drawing plans
page 28

Repairing wiring
page 30

WIRING A KITCHEN

Electrical services abound in modern kitchens: lights on the ceiling; lights in, on, and under cabinets; counter receptacles with the capacity to run six or seven appliances at once; and separate circuits for appliances such as the refrigerator, dishwasher, and microwave. All in all, a medium-size kitchen may require six, seven, or more circuits.

Types of lighting

General lighting (or ambient lighting) is usually provided by ceiling-mounted fixtures. Consider fluorescent fixtures with "daylight" tubes and opaque lenses to disperse the light. Or install a series of recessed canister lights or incandescent fixtures.

If you use a track fixture for general lighting, shown on the opposite page, you'll get better illumination if you run several tracks around the room rather than having a single track in the middle. That way the light comes from several different directions.

Cove lighting mounts on top of wall cabinets and points upward, providing general lighting and creating a halo effect.

Area lighting focuses on a certain spot while also providing some general illumination. A recessed canister light equipped with a spotlight bulb, for instance, may shine down on the sink. Be sure to position it so the person doing dishes does not cast a shadow over the work area.

Pendant shade lights, as shown, are ideal area lights placed over a dining table or a counter. Position them over the center of the table or counter and adjust the heights so they do not shine in people's eyes.

Task lighting directs a beam of light at a work surface. The position of task lighting is critical: It must be in front of the worker to eliminate shadows, but it must not shine in the worker's eyes. Fortunately, a perfect location is available in almost every kitchen: the underside of wall cabinets. Undercabinet lights are available as fluorescent or low-voltage halogen fixtures.

Accent lighting shines a spotlight on an object, such as a wall hanging. As shown, small fluorescent lights inside a glass-doored cabinet draw attention to a collection of fine china and crystal.

Consider installing a grow-light pointed at decorative or culinary plants. The one shown here shines on an herb garden positioned in front of the window. A typical grow-light cannot supply plants with all the rays they need, but it can be a supplement.

Light switches

Think carefully about the location of switches. If you put four or five next to each other, people may be confused about which switch controls which light. Where possible, position switches near their lights.

Be sure that you can turn on lights easily, no matter which door or entryway you use. Often the most convenient arrangement is to use three-way switches so that a single light or series of lights can be controlled by two different switches (*pages 70–73*).

The lights in a kitchen typically are on a single 15-amp circuit.

Receptacles

Codes often require that a refrigerator receptacle be on a separate circuit because a blown circuit breaker or fuse could lead to food spoiling. A microwave oven may need its own circuit too, depending on its size and power.

Most codes require two circuits for countertop receptacles. In some areas, the receptacles must be ground fault circuits (GFCI receptacles, *page 59*) and must be on 20-amp alternating circuits (*page 62*). In other areas, the required arrangement is to have two 15-amp circuits with non-GFCI receptacles wired with split circuits so the two plugs are connected to two different circuits (*page 63*). Check local codes.

Appliances

An electric range, cooktop, or oven must be wired to a dedicated 120/240-volt circuit (*page 60*). Other appliances are 120-volt.

Under the sink, there must be a receptacle for the garbage disposer. It may be split so that one plug is switched and the other is always hot (*page 64*), allowing you to plug in a garbage disposer and a hot-water dispenser. Or the disposer may be hardwired into a switched box. The switch is usually placed on the wall near the sink.

A dishwasher may have its own circuit, or it may be on the same circuit as the garbage disposer. A range hood (*pages 91–93*) typically is hardwired.

Over-sink canister light

Cove lighting

Grow-light

Switch for garbage disposer

Wire for dishwasher and disposer under the sink.

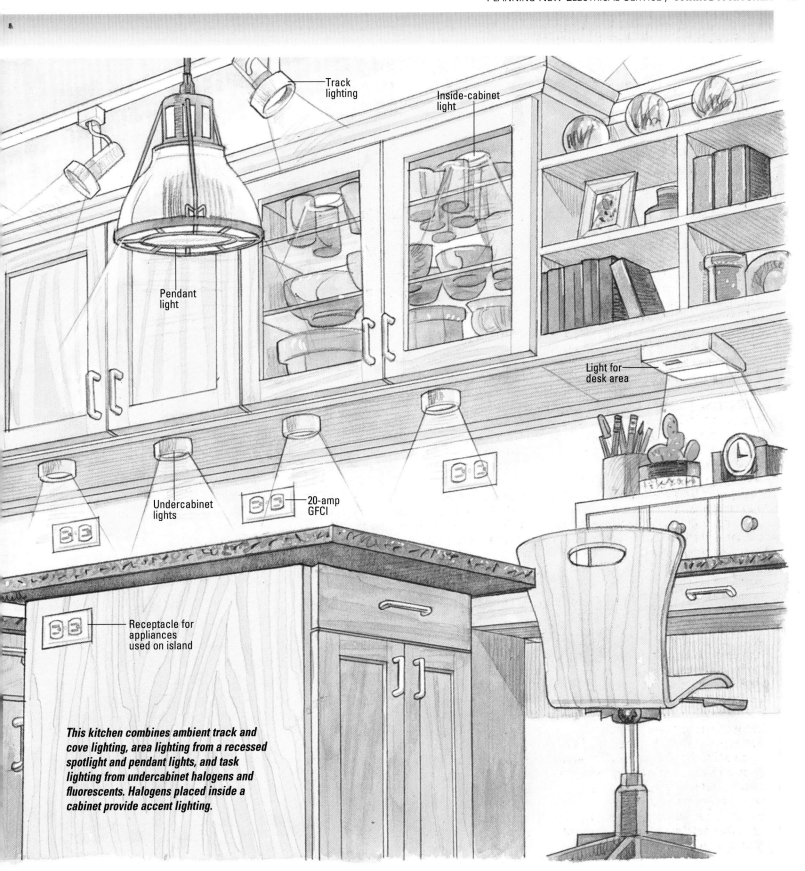

Track lighting

Inside-cabinet light

Pendant light

Light for desk area

Undercabinet lights

20-amp GFCI

Receptacle for appliances used on island

This kitchen combines ambient track and cove lighting, area lighting from a recessed spotlight and pendant lights, and task lighting from undercabinet halogens and fluorescents. Halogens placed inside a cabinet provide accent lighting.

WIRING A BATHROOM

Even a relatively large bathroom tends to be damp. Light fixtures must be watertight, ventilation must be effective, and the receptacles should be ground fault circuit interrupters.

Circuits
The lights and fan must be on a different circuit from the receptacle(s). Some codes require that bathrooms have their own circuits; others permit bathrooms to share circuits with receptacles or lights in other rooms. In some locales, all bathroom wiring—including the lights—must be GFCI-protected *(pages 59 and 113)*.

The vent fan
To satisfy codes and for your comfort, a bathroom needs a fan that effectively pulls moist air out and sends it outside. *Pages 94–97* show how to install one. Some local codes require that the fan always come on when the light is on; others allow you to put the fan on its own switch.

Usually, there is a vent/light fixture in the middle of the ceiling, which may be controlled by one or two switches. Some fixtures also include a heating unit or a night-light. A bathroom heater—whether it is a separate unit or a part of a fan/light—may use so much electricity that it requires its own circuit.

Lights
In addition to a light or fan/light in the middle of the ceiling, plan to put lights over the sink, where they can shine on a person standing at the mirror. A strip of lights above the mirror is a common arrangement, but most people find that two lights, one on each side of the mirror, illuminate a face more clearly. A mirror light's switch may be by the entry door or near the sink.

A tub or shower does not need to be brightly lit, but people shouldn't have to shower in the dark. Install a recessed canister light with a waterproof lens made for shower areas.

Receptacles
Install at least one 20-amp GFCI receptacle within a foot or so of the sink. Position the receptacle so a cord does not have to drape over the sink when someone is using a blow dryer.

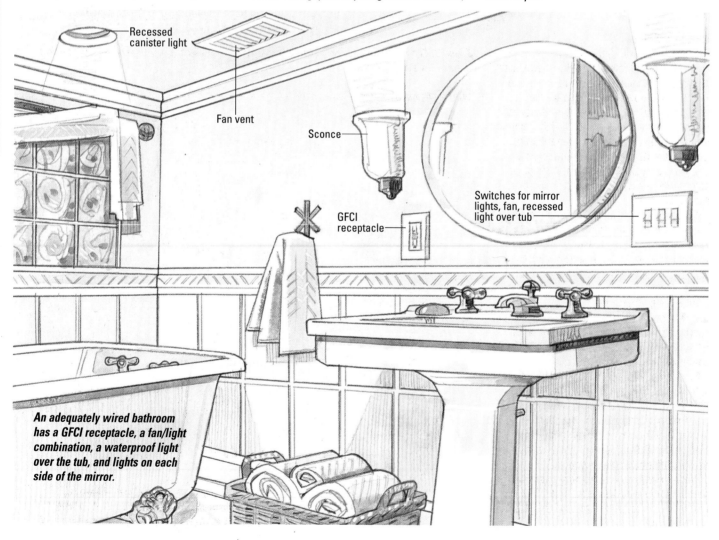

Recessed canister light

Fan vent

Sconce

GFCI receptacle

Switches for mirror lights, fan, recessed light over tub

An adequately wired bathroom has a GFCI receptacle, a fan/light combination, a waterproof light over the tub, and lights on each side of the mirror.

WIRING UTILITY ROOMS

Work areas tend to be informal, with unfinished walls and exposed framing. Unfortunately, the wiring is sometimes just as informal with exposed cable, overloaded receptacles, missing coverplates, and a tangle of extension cords.

Safe utility wiring

Attach all boxes firmly, and staple or strap cables so they are taut and out of harm's way. Although some codes allow it, exposed NM cable is unsafe in an area where people work. Replace it with armored cable or conduit *(pages 36–41)*.

Make sure there are enough receptacles placed in convenient locations to avoid the need for long extension cords. You shouldn't have to use three-way adapters. If the area is damp, install GFCIs.

Wiring a workshop

People will be wielding tools and moving large pieces of lumber, so take special care in placing the receptacles. In a large shop with serious power tools, add up the amperages to see if one or two dedicated circuits are needed *(pages 24–25)*. Position a receptacle near each stationary power tool, such as a table saw or drill press. Scatter plenty of other receptacles so you can plug in hand power tools without using extension cords.

Provide plenty of overhead lighting. Large fluorescent fixtures do the trick easily and inexpensively. Install lenses to cover the tubes to prevent breakage. For work that requires close scrutiny, plug in desk lamps.

Wiring a laundry room

Codes are very specific about laundry room requirements. Use common sense when positioning receptacles so that cords are well away from the folding table.

If the dryer is electric, you need a separate 120/240-volt receptacle *(pages 60–61)*. If the dryer is gas, it can plug into a receptacle on the same circuit as the washer. There should be an extra receptacle so you won't have to reach back and unplug the washer or dryer when you need power.

The receptacles in a laundry room must be on a dedicated 20-amp circuit. The lights, however, can share a circuit with lights in another room.

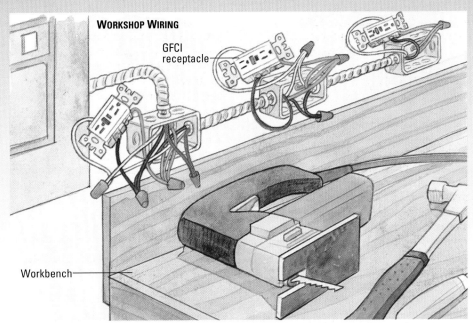

WORKSHOP WIRING

GFCI receptacle

Workbench

These GFCI receptacles, spaced about a foot apart, are on alternating circuits (page 62) *so that there is little chance of overloading.*

LAUNDRY ROOM WIRING

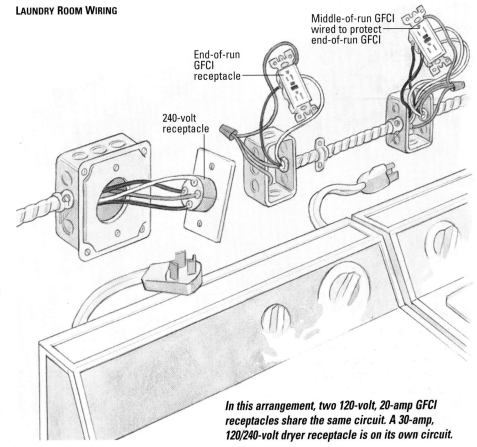

Middle-of-run GFCI wired to protect end-of-run GFCI

End-of-run GFCI receptacle

240-volt receptacle

In this arrangement, two 120-volt, 20-amp GFCI receptacles share the same circuit. A 30-amp, 120/240-volt dryer receptacle is on its own circuit.

CODES OFTEN ENCOUNTERED

If you're simply replacing an existing fixture, switch, or receptacle, there's usually no need to contact the building department. But when you run new electrical cable for new service, whether wiring several circuits or adding just one receptacle, be sure to work with a building inspector and comply with all local codes.

National and local codes
Professional electricians often refer to the National Electrical Code (NEC), a massive volume that describes national codes for residential and commercial wiring. You don't need to buy this book, but you may need to refer to a library copy from time to time.

Local building departments often modify the NEC, and it is local codes that you must satisfy. It's not unusual for adjacent towns to have very different codes; for instance, one may allow plastic boxes while another requires metal boxes.

The charts in this section present many of the most important code requirements. However, they are not exhaustive. **Have your wiring plans approved by a local inspector before you begin work.**

If existing wiring does not meet contemporary local codes, chances are that your building department will not require you to change the wiring. Usually only the new work must be up to code. However, if the old wiring is unsafe, you should change it. An extensive remodeling project may also require you to bring the entire house up to current codes.

Loading and grounding circuits
Any plan, however simple or complex, must start with two considerations. First, make sure the new service will not overload a circuit. *Pages 24–25* explain how.

Second, see that all receptacles and appliances are safely grounded. Local codes will probably require that switches and light fixtures also be grounded. Grounding provides protection against shock in case a wire comes loose or an appliance or device malfunctions. Check using a receptacle analyzer *(page 8)*.

All receptacles and appliances must be attached to a ground wire (or metal sheathing) that runs to the service panel. The most common methods of grounding are shown below. Check with local codes to find out which method they approve.

A thick ground wire should emerge from the service panel and clamp tightly to a cold-water pipe or grounding rods driven into the ground outside the house.

Common code requirements

Here are some of the most common general requirements for home electrical systems. Keep in mind that local building departments may have different demands.

■ **Boxes:** Plastic electrical boxes are common throughout much of the United States and Canada; some localities require metal boxes. Buy large boxes so wires won't be cramped *(page 13)*. Attach them firmly to a framing member whenever possible or use remodel boxes that clamp to the wall surface *(pages 48–49)*.

■ **Receptacles, fixtures, and appliances:** All new receptacles and appliances must be grounded. Fixtures and appliances should be approved by the Underwriter's Laboratory (UL).

■ **Cable:** Nonmetallic (NM) cable is the easiest to run and is accepted by most building departments. Wherever cable will be exposed rather than hidden behind drywall or plaster, armored cable or conduit may be required. See Chapter Three for the correct ways to install cable, so it is protected against harm.

■ **Circuits:** Most 120-volt household circuits are 15 amps, and all lights must be on 15-amp circuits. In kitchens and utility areas, 20-amp circuits may be required. To make sure your circuits aren't overloaded, *see pages 24–25*.

■ **Wire size.** Attach #14 wire to 15-amp circuits and #12 wire to 20-amp circuits. If cable runs exceed 500 feet, you may need to increase wire size. Consult your building department.

■ **Service panels:** As long as you do not need to add a new circuit *(pages 112–113)*, your existing service panel, even if it is an old fuse box, will probably be sufficient. If you add circuits, you may need to upgrade the panel or add a subpanel *(pages 114–115)*. Check with an inspector.

REFRESHER COURSE
Grounding methods

If the box is plastic, connect the ground wire to the receptacle only. For a middle of-the-run receptacle *(shown)* splice the ground wires together and connect to the receptacle with a pigtail.

With a metal box, attach ground wires to both the receptacle and to the box using a grounding screw. Use a pigtail and a grounding wire nut.

Systems that use armored cable or metal conduit may have no grounding wire. The sheathing or conduit provides the path for ground, so it must be connected firmly at all points.

STANLEY PRO TIP

Working with the electrical inspector

Filing for a permit and working with an electrical inspector may seem unnecessary, but the inspection process ensures safe and reliable electrical service. Most inspectors know their business; pay attention and follow their instructions to the letter. You will benefit from the sound advice.

■ **Find out if your building department requires a licensed electrician** to perform new electrical installations. Some departments require a homeowner to pass a written or oral test before performing doing certain types of work.

■ **Make a rough sketch and materials list** for the project before you start drawing plans and then find out as much as possible about local codes. Find out what kind of cable and boxes are required. Are there any specific requirements for the room you will be wiring? The building department may have pamphlets answering your questions, or an inspector may be able to answer them over the phone.

■ **The inspector's job is not to help you plan, but to inspect.** An inspector may be willing to offer advice, but don't ask, "What should I do?" Instead, propose a plan using the information in this chapter and present it for feedback.

■ **Draw up professional-looking plans** (pages 28–29), as well as a complete list of materials. Make an appointment with the inspector to go over your plans. Listen attentively and take notes. Be polite and respectful, but don't be afraid to ask questions if you don't understand.

■ **Schedule inspections.** There will probably be two: one for the rough wiring and one for the finished job. Don't call the inspector in until the required work is completely finished—inspectors hate having to come back for a reinspection. Above all, do not cover up any wiring until the inspector has signed off on it. If you install drywall before the rough electrical inspection, you may have to tear it off.

Electrical codes room by room

Some codes apply to the entire house; others apply to specific rooms. Here are some general guidelines. Local codes may vary. These requirements usually apply only to new installations—older wiring does not have to comply as long as it is safe. These requirements make good sense and are not overly strict. Wiring that does not meet these standards would be either awkward or unsafe to use.

Bedrooms, living room, dining room

Every room in a house must have a wall switch located near the entry door, which controls either a ceiling fixture or a switched receptacle. All ceiling fixtures must be controlled by a wall switch and not by a pull chain. Receptacles must be no more than 12 feet apart, and there must be at least one on each wall. If a section of wall between two doors is wider than 2 feet, it must have a receptacle. Light fixtures must be on 15-amp circuits. Usually receptacles are allowed to share a circuit with lights. But a heavy electrical user, such as a window air-conditioner or a home theater, may need to be on a dedicated circuit.

Hallways and stairways

All stairways must have a light fixture controlled by three-way switches at the bottom and top of the stairs. Hallways may also need a light controlled by three-ways. A hallway longer than 10 feet must have at least one receptacle.

Closets

There should be at least one overhead light, controlled by a wall switch rather than a pull-chain. The light must have a globe rather than a bare bulb; a bulb can get hot enough to ignite clothing, stacked blankets, or storage boxes.

Attached garage

There must be at least one receptacle—not counting receptacles used for laundry or other utilities. There should be an overhead light (in addition to a light that is part of a garage door opener) controlled by at least one wall switch.

Kitchen

Here things can get pretty complicated; see pages 18–19. Many codes call for two 20-amp small appliance circuits, controlling GFCI receptacles placed above countertops. Other codes call for 15-amp split-circuit receptacles. The refrigerator, microwave, garbage disposer, and dishwasher may or may not need to be on separate circuits. The lights should be on a separate 15-amp circuit.

Bathroom

Codes require that all receptacles be GFCI-protected. Any light fixture should have sealed globe or lens to seal out moisture. A fan/light/heater may pull enough amps to require its own circuit.

Outdoors

For standard-voltage wiring, codes call for either waterproof underground feed (UF) cable or conduit, or both. The depth at which the cable must be buried varies depending on local codes. Special waterproof fittings and covers are called for. For low-voltage lighting, standards are less strict; usually no permit is needed for installation.

LOADING CIRCUITS FOR SAFETY

When adding only a few receptacles, lights, or a small appliance, tap into an existing circuit. Grab power from a nearby receptacle, junction box, switch box, or ceiling fixture box *(pages 42–43)* and run cable to the new electrical box. First make sure that you won't overload the circuit.

Indexing circuits

An index telling which electrical users—lights, receptacles, and appliances—are on each circuit should be posted on the inside of a service panel door. However, this index may not be accurate. Whenever evaluating a circuit, **test to make sure which electrical users are on the circuit.**

If there is no index, make one. Shut off one circuit and test to see which lights, receptacles, or appliances have been turned off. Write down the results. Repeat for all the circuits until you have covered all electrical users in the house. Draw up the index and tape it to the service panel.

Indexing circuits is easier with two people, one stationed at the service panel while the other tests plugs, lights, and appliances and writes down the findings. Walkie-talkies or a pair of cell phones ease communications.

Figuring the load

Once you've identified all the users on a circuit, total up the wattage. If the wattage is not printed on an item's label, there should be an amperage rating (amps). For 120-volt users, multiply the amps times 120 to get the wattage. For example, a 4-amp tool uses 480 watts ($4 \times 120 = 480$).

Add the wattage of all the bulbs in each fixture. For each receptacle, include the appliances or tools that are commonly plugged into them. (Don't forget the vacuum cleaner.) Also include hardwired appliances such as a dishwasher. Once you've totaled all the electrical users on a circuit, determine if adding new services will overload the circuit. The box *(above right)* shows how to make this calculation. If grabbing power from a nearby box will overload its circuit, try another circuit. If no convenient circuit has enough available capacity, install a new circuit *(pages 26–27)*.

Major appliances such as electric ranges and dryers use dedicated 240-volt circuits. Only one user is connected to each circuit.

Calculating safe capacity for a circuit

To find the total capacity of a circuit, multiply amps times volts (usually 120). Most local codes demand that all the users on a circuit must not add up to more than 80 percent of total capacity. This 80-percent figure is the circuit's "safe capacity."

15-amp circuit
total capacity: 1800 watts
safe capacity: 1440 watts (12 amps)

20-amp circuit
total capacity: 2400 watts
safe capacity: 1920 watts (16 amps)

30-amp circuit
total capacity: 3600 watts
safe capacity: 2880 watts (24 amps)

REFRESHER COURSE
Home electrical circuits

Power from the utility company enters the service panel, where it is divided into individual "branch" circuits, each of which supplies power to specific lights, receptacles, or appliances. In each circuit, a black or colored hot wire carries power out to the user, and a white neutral wire completes the circuit by carrying power back to the service panel.

Some household electrical systems are orderly with each circuit covering a clearly defined area of the house. Others are helter-skelter—a single circuit may travel across the house or up two floors. Disorganized wiring is not necessarily unsafe, but it may take extra time to figure out what's going on when you add new service or track down a problem.

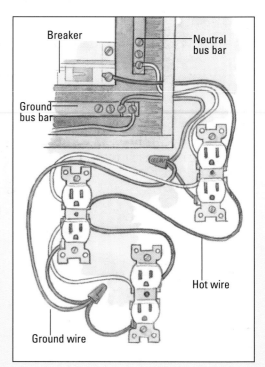

Breaker
Neutral bus bar
Ground bus bar
Hot wire
Ground wire

Appliances and tools that need special attention

To find the wattage of a 120-volt appliance or tool, look at its nameplate. If it tells only the amps, multiply times 120 to get the wattage. For example, a table saw that pulls 11 amps uses 1320 watts (11 × 120 = 1320). Here are some typical wattages; yours may vary considerably. (All 240-volt appliances should be on dedicated circuits, so you never need to figure whether they can fit in a circuit.)

Television, 350 watts

Table saw, 800–1400 watts

Window air-conditioner, 700–1600 watts

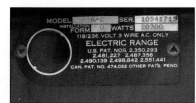

Electric range, 4000–4500

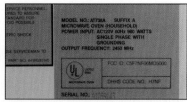

Microwave, 600–1500 watts

Dishwasher, 1000–1500 watts

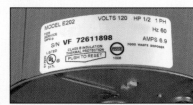

Garbage disposer, 400–850 watts

Hair dryer, 500–1200 watts

Refrigerator, 800–1200 watts

Ways to relieve an overloaded circuit

If a circuit often blows a fuse or trips a breaker, it means too many appliances, lights, or tools are sharing it. List the wattage ratings of all the electrical users on the circuit. Add up the numbers, and the total will probably exceed safe capacity (left).

The solution may be as simple as plugging an appliance into a nearby receptacle that is on another circuit. If that is not possible, install a wall-mounted extension cord (center) or protective channel (right) so you can plug the device into a receptacle located on another circuit.

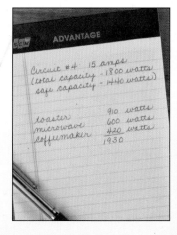

Wall-mounted extension cord

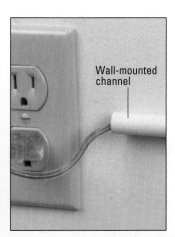

Wall-mounted channel

CHECKING OUT YOUR BASIC SERVICE

Installing a new circuit is not difficult. First make sure that your service panel can handle the extra load. A service panel with too many circuits is dangerous.

Fuse boxes rarely have space for new circuits. If you have a fuse box and need new service, replace it with a new service panel or install a subpanel (pages 114–115).

If you see an available slot in a breaker box, either an open space or a knockout that can be removed, chances are you can simply install a new breaker there and run cable to it. If there is no open space, local codes may allow you to replace a single breaker with a tandem breaker, which supplies power to two circuits (pages 112–113).

Make sure you will not overload your service panel. A panel's total amperage is printed near or on the main circuit breaker, which controls all the circuits in the panel. Most breaker boxes are 100, 150, or 200 amps. Add the amperages of all the individual breakers in the box. The total may be more than twice the total amperage of the box. For example, a 100-amp service panel may have circuits that add up to over 200 amps. This is normal.

Take your total amperages and the name of the service panel manufacturer with you to meet with the inspector to ask about adding another circuit. Or compute your home's power needs using the chart at right.

Evaluating a home's total loads

A 60-amp service is probably too little for a modern home unless it is small. If a home is under 3,000 square feet and does not have central air-conditioning or electric heat, 100-amp service should be enough. A home larger than 2,000 square feet with central air or electric heat probably needs 200-amp service.

1. Calculate your total needs. First multiply the square footage of all the living areas times three watts. This is the total lighting and receptacle needs.

2. Add 1500 watts for each kitchen small-appliance circuit and laundry-room circuit.

3. Add the wattages for all appliances that are on their own circuits, such as an electric dryer, water heater, or range; or a window air-conditioner. (Check the nameplates and remember that watts = volts times amps.)

4. Add the three numbers up. Figure the first 10,000 watts at 100 percent and the remaining watts at 40 percent.

5. Add the wattage of either the heating unit or the central air-conditioner—whichever is greater.

6. Divide this figure by 230. This figure tells how many amps a home needs.

Example

Here's a sample calculation for a 2,000-square-foot home with central air:

1. 2,000 square feet × 3 =	6,000 watts
2. Two kitchen small-appliance circuits plus a laundry-room circuit: 3 × 1500 =	4,500 watts
3. Water heater: 5,000 watts	
Dishwasher: 1,200 watts	
Electric dryer: 5,500 watts =	11,700 watts
	22,200 watts
4. First 10,000 at 100 percent =	10,000 watts
Remaining 12,200 at 40 percent =	4,800 watts
Subtotal =	**14,880 watts**
5. Central air =	4,000 watts
Total =	**18,800 watts**
6. Total divided by 230 =	÷ 230
(100-amp service will be enough for this home.)	**81 amps**

REFRESHER COURSE
Inspecting a service panel

A service panel should be located out of children's reach, but where adults can get to it easily. Any exposed cables leading to it should be firmly attached to the wall and clamped tightly to knockout holes in the panel. If there are any open holes, cover them with a "goof plug" (available at hardware stores).

If a #14 wire is connected to a 20-amp circuit breaker or fuse, replace the breaker or fuse with one that is 15 amps to prevent the wire from overheating. In most cases, a 20-amp fuse or breaker should be connected to a #12 wire; a 30-amp fuse or breaker should be connected to a #10 wire.

Wires should run in a fairly orderly way around the perimeter of the panel. If you find a hopeless tangle, call in an electrician for evaluation. Also call in a pro if you find melted or nicked wire insulation, any signs of fire, or extensive rust.

In an older home, there's a good chance that a service panel has had new wiring added over the years—perhaps by a pro, perhaps by an amateur. So check out all the connections.

Small fuse box: A 60-amp fuse box may be found in an older home that has not had its wiring upgraded. It can supply power to only one 240-volt appliance and is probably inadequate for a home larger than 1,200 square feet.

Medium size service: A 100-amp service panel provides enough power for a medium-sized home, even if it has several 240-volt appliances and central air-conditioning (opposite page).

Large capacity: Many newer homes and some older large homes have a 150- or 200-amp service panel. Unless the home is a mansion, there is virtually no way to overload it.

STANLEY PRO TIP: **Making room in a service panel**

Knockout tab

If a service panel has an unused slot for a circuit breaker, installing a new breaker is easy. Poke and twist out the knockout tab and install the new breaker (pages 112–113).

Tandem breaker

If there is no open space, codes may permit you to replace a single breaker with a tandem breaker, which supplies two circuits while taking up only one space. Ask an inspector.

Add capacity with a subpanel

Subpanel

If you can't fit new breakers into the service panel, either hire a pro to install a new service panel or add a subpanel. Pages 114–115 show you how to do this.

DRAWING PLANS

Carefully drawn plans help show the building inspector that you've thought through your project. And spending an extra hour or two with pencil and paper will help you spot potential problems before you begin tearing into walls, saving you time and expense in the long run.

A drawing must include the locations and types of all fixtures, switches, receptacles, hardwired appliances, and cables. On an attached sheet, provide a complete list of materials.

Drawing plans

Get a pad of graph paper, a straightedge, a compass, and several colored pencils if you will be installing several circuits. Make a scale drawing of the room, including features such as counters and cabinets.

First make a rough drawing. Use the symbols shown below or get a list of symbols from your local building department. Make a quick freehand drawing, using colored pencils to indicate each circuit. Are the switches in convenient locations? Are all the circuits correctly loaded *(pages 24–25)*? Do you have enough receptacles, and will they be easy to reach? Once you've made your final decisions, draw a neat, final version of the plan.

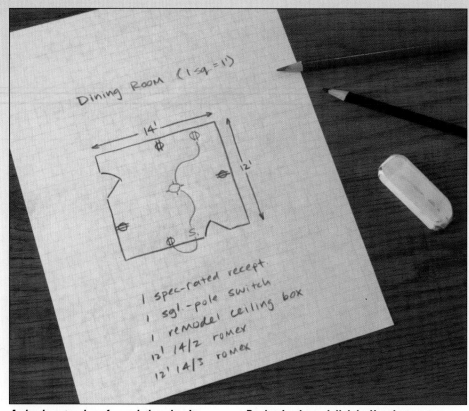

A simple extension of an existing circuit— in this example, adding a receptacle and a switched light fixture—is easy to draw.

Don't take the task lightly: Use the correct symbols and make the drawing clear and neat.

Electrical symbols

		◯		⊕
Duplex receptacle	240-volt receptacle	Ceiling light fixture	Split-wired duplex receptacle	Fourplex receptacle
	Ⓙ	CF	VF	S
Wall light	Wall junction box	Ceiling fan	Vent fan	Switched receptacle
	Ⓡ	GFCI	▷|	TV
Fluorescent ceiling light	Recessed canister light	GFCI receptacle	Indoor telephone	Television jack
	S	S$_P$	S$_3$	S$_4$
Service panel	Single-pole switch	Pilot light switch	3-way switch	4-way switch

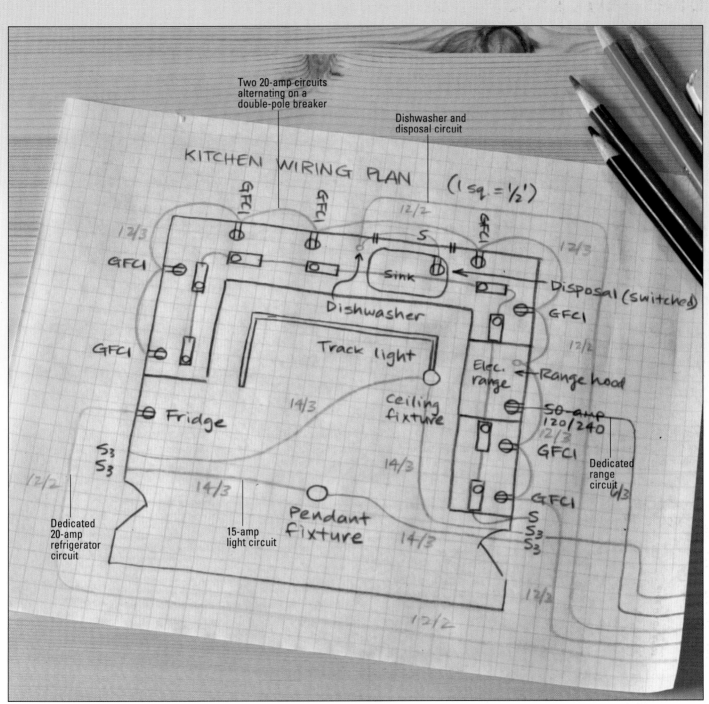

Safe capacity

To make sure the planned circuits won't be overloaded, check *page 24* for how to calculate safe capacity.

Photocopy the floor plan

For complex projects, draw your floor plan, then make several photocopies. This allows you to sketch out several trial plans.

This plan for wiring a kitchen includes a 15-amp circuit for lights, some controlled by three-way switches. A 15-amp refrigerator circuit has been added, as well as two 20-amp small-appliance circuits and a 20-amp circuit for the dishwasher and garbage disposer. The range has its own circuit.

REPAIRING WIRING

Whenever you untangle a wire splice or disconnect a wire from a terminal, you rebend a wire and thereby weaken it. To make sure it will not break and cause a splice or connection to fail, follow the wire handling steps at right.

Wire repair tips

■ If wire insulation is generally brittle and/or cracked, purchase hot-shrink sleeves, designed to reinsulate wires. They're available in little bags at hardware stores and home centers. Slip a sleeve over the damaged wire and aim a heat gun at it until the sleeve shrinks and molds itself to the wire.

■ If bare wire shows below a wire nut, remove the nut, snip the bare wire(s) to shorten it slightly, and reinstall the nut.

■ If a wire's insulation is nicked near the point where it enters a box, it may be difficult to reach the damaged area with tape. Try slipping on a red plastic armored cable bushing *(page 37)*.

Keeping boxes safe

If the front edge of a box is recessed behind the wall surface more than ¼ inch (this commonly happens when a wall is covered with paneling or tiling), it is considered unsafe and out of code. Box extenders solve the problem. They're available for boxes of every size and are easy to install.

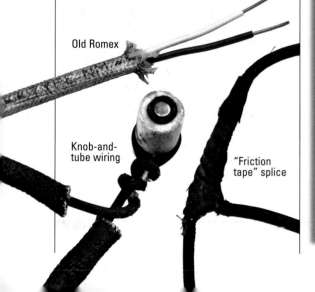

Old Romex

Knob-and-tube wiring

"Friction tape" splice

Repairing wiring in boxes

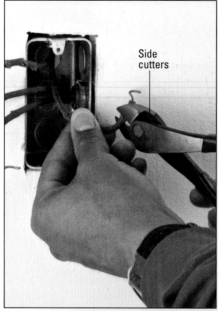

Side cutters

Cut, strip: Turn off power and test for power in the box. After disconnecting wire from a splice or terminal, snip off all the exposed wire, using side cutters, lineman's pliers, or strippers. Strip off ¾ inch of insulation to connect to a terminal or 1 inch of insulation to make a splice.

Heat-shrink tubing

Heat gun

Cover with tubing: If wiring is damaged, use heat-shrink tubing to cover old insulation. Cut the tubing to length, slip it over the damaged wire, and heat the tubing until it shrinks tight around the wire.

Evaluating old wire and cable

Old Romex or knob-and-tube wiring (left) may have cloth insulation that can crack with age. Particularly with knob-and-tube, splices may be covered with clothlike "friction tape" (below left). As long as the insulation is sound and the splice is covered, it is safe. If a tape-covered splice is coming unraveled, remove the tape and twist on a wire nut.

Old wiring may be so dirty that you cannot tell hot (black) wires from neutral (formerly white) wires. It is important to find out—if you connect the neutral wire rather than the hot wire to a switch, power will always be present in the box, even when the switch is off. Gently clean portions of old insulation, using a cloth dampened with alcohol or soapy water, until you can tell which wire has white insulation.

STANLEY PRO TIP

Snip wires before removing

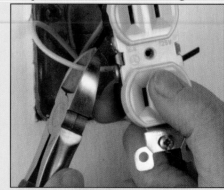

Rather than disconnecting a device and then repairing wire ends, save time by simply cutting the wires just behind the terminals. Then strip and reconnect. Make sure remaining wires will be long enough—6 to 8 inches—before you cut.

Grounding an old receptacle

Knockout slug

New ground wire

Fish tape

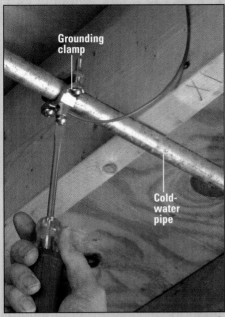

Grounding clamp

Cold-water pipe

1 If you have an old system with ungrounded receptacles and want to ground one receptacle, **shut off power to the circuit, test for power,** and pull out the receptacle. Pry out a knockout slug and then twist it back and forth to remove it.

2 Use the techniques shown on *pages 50–53* to make a pathway for a ground wire. Use one or two fish tapes to run a #12 green-insulated wire from the box to the service panel or to a cold-water pipe.

3 Connect the wire to the ground screw of the receptacle. Connect the other end to a cold-water pipe with a special grounding clamp.

STANLEY PRO TIP

Test a two-hole receptacle for grounding

If your system has two-hole receptacles, it is probably an ungrounded system. To make sure, shut off power, pull out a receptacle, and restore power. Insert one probe of a voltage tester into the hot (shorter) slot of the receptacle, and touch the other probe to the metal box. If the tester doesn't light, the system is not grounded. However, if it lights, the box is grounded; you can install a three-hole (grounded) receptacle and run a ground wire from the receptacle grounding terminal to a grounding screw in the box. Test the new receptacle for ground using a receptacle analyzer *(page 8)*.

Tricks for replacing cable

Wire insulation inside boxes (especially ceiling boxes, which get hot) deteriorates faster than wire wrapped inside cable. So even if you find a lot of brittle insulation inside a box, the wiring hidden inside your walls is probably OK. However, if you find brittle insulation in several boxes, call in a pro for an evaluation; the wiring in your house may need to be replaced.

Rewiring a house is usually a job for professionals; but if you work systematically and with your building department's approval, you may attempt it. The safest way is to pull and replace one cable at a time.

Running cable and connecting wires will probably be less than half the work. Cutting walls and ceilings to get at the cable, and patching and painting afterwards, will take much more time.

If you have exposed cable (for example, in a basement or attic), start by replacing it. Refer to *pages 50–53* for methods of running cable through walls.

In some cases, you may be able to pull cable through a wall or ceiling without damaging it. Once you've discovered where a cable leads (for example, between two receptacles) disconnect the cable at both ends. At one end, tightly tape the new cable to the old cable, making the splice as thin as possible so it can run through tight holes. Pull on the other end, and if you're lucky, the new cable will come through. Unfortunately sometimes there are tight turns or the cable is stapled, so this technique does not work and you will have to cut into the wall or ceiling.

INSTALLING CABLES & BOXES

In a typical wiring project, installing cable and boxes can take four or five times as long as making the connections. It's important to plan cable runs and box placement carefully.

Getting the right materials
All the materials you plan to install need the approval of your local building department. Local electrical codes will determine the type of cable you need, as well as whether the boxes should be plastic or metal. Buy boxes that are as large as possible or consult *page 13* to make sure your boxes are large enough for the wires they will hold.

Cable, boxes, receptacles, and switches are not expensive and can be returned if you do not use them. So buy more than you think you need to save trips back to the home center. Purchase plenty of the little items needed for a project too—straps or staples, nail guards, electrician's tape, and wire nuts of several sizes.

Plan your work
Be sure you understand exactly how each installation will be wired. Consult the specific projects described in this book. Follow them from start to finish. Draw a plan and make a materials list. Have them approved by your local building department. Buy all the materials you need and store them in an uncluttered space so you can easily get at what you need when you need it.

The order of work
Determine how you will connect to power *(pages 42–43)*. When working in exposed framing (in a new addition, or if the drywall or plaster has been removed), first install the boxes, then drill holes and run the cable *(pages 44–47)*.

If you are working in finished walls and ceilings, first cut holes for the boxes *(page 48)*. Run the cable through a basement or attic or fish it through the walls *(pages 50–53)*. Then install the boxes *(page 49)*.

Here's how to install the backbone of a new circuit—boxes to hold devices and cable to carry power.

CHAPTER PREVIEW

Nonmetallic (NM) cable
page 34

Armored cable
page 36

Metal conduit
page 38

PVC conduit
page 40

Pulling wires
page 41

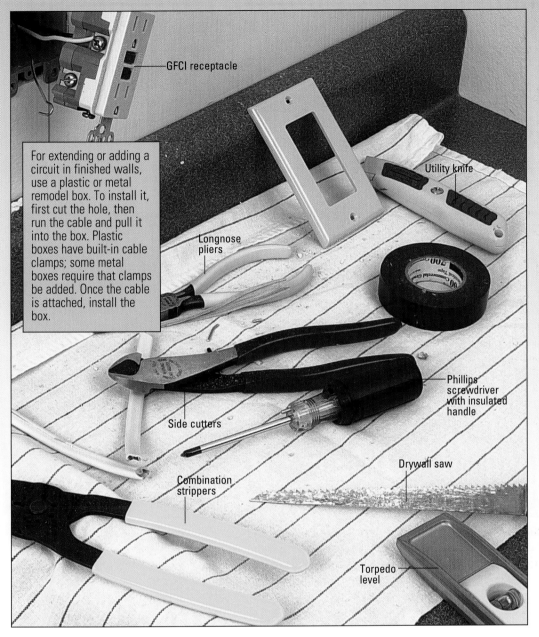

GFCI receptacle

For extending or adding a circuit in finished walls, use a plastic or metal remodel box. To install it, first cut the hole, then run the cable and pull it into the box. Plastic boxes have built-in cable clamps; some metal boxes require that clamps be added. Once the cable is attached, install the box.

Utility knife

Longnose pliers

Phillips screwdriver with insulated handle

Side cutters

Combination strippers

Drywall saw

Torpedo level

To attach a new receptacle or switch, start by removing sheathing from cable (pages 34–37) and strip wire ends—1 inch for a splice, or ¾ inch for a terminal connection—using a pair of combination strippers. Poke the stripped wires into the box and clamp the cable. If you need to splice two or more wires, hold them side by side, grab their ends with a pair of lineman's pliers, and twist them together to form a uniform spiral. Snip off the end and twist on a wire nut of the correct size (page 15). To connect a wire to a terminal, use longnose pliers or a wire-bending screwdriver to form a clockwise loop in the wire end. Slip the loop over a loosened terminal screw, squeeze the wire tight to the screw threads, and tighten the screw.

Grabbing power
page 42

Installing boxes
page 44

Running cable
page 45

Steel studs
page 47

Finished walls
page 48

Finished rooms
page 50

Patching walls
page 54

STRIPPING AND CLAMPING NM CABLE

Nonmetallic cable (NM cable) is easy to work with and inexpensive, so it's not surprising that it is the most common type of cable used in household wiring.

NM cable is usually sold in lengths of 25, 50, or 100 feet, or more. When in doubt, buy the larger package—it doesn't cost much more and it may come in handy later.

NM's plastic sheathing does not offer much protection to the wires, so keep it out of harm's way. If the cable might get wet, install UF (underground feed) cable, which encases wires in molded plastic. Wherever cable will be exposed—in a garage or basement—many local codes call for armored cable or conduit *(pages 38–41)*.

Codes call for running NM through the center of studs so that drywall nails cannot damage it. If the cable is less than 1¼ inches from the edge of a framing member, install a protective metal plate *(page 46)*. Some codes require metal plates even if the cable is in the center of a stud.

Take care not to damage wire insulation when working with NM cable. Slit the sheathing right down the middle using a sharp utility knife. Don't cut too deep to avoid slicing the wire insulation. Or use the sheathing stripper shown below.

When cutting cable to length, leave yourself an extra foot or two. If you make a mistake while stripping, you can recut the cable and try again.

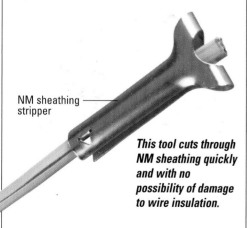

NM sheathing stripper

This tool cuts through NM sheathing quickly and with no possibility of damage to wire insulation.

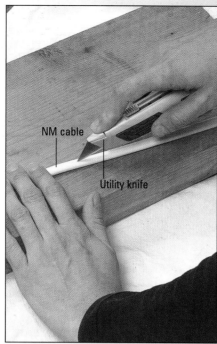

NM cable

Utility knife

1 Lay the cable on a flat work surface, such as a small sheet of plywood. Starting 8 to 10 inches from the end, insert the tip of a utility knife blade into the center of the cable, pushing just hard enough to cut through the sheathing.

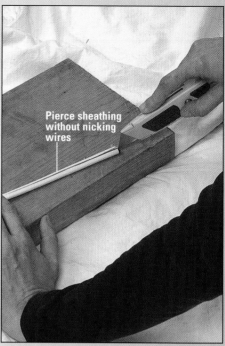

Pierce sheathing without nicking wires

2 Slice the sheathing, exerting even pressure. You'll feel the tip of the knife rubbing against the bare ground wire as you slice. With practice, you can cut evenly and quickly without damaging wire insulation.

WHAT IF ...
You have 3-wire cable?

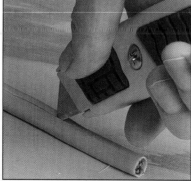

NM cable that holds three wires (plus the ground) is round rather than flat. If you cut through the sheathing too deeply, you'll hit insulated wire rather than the ground wire. Practice cutting through the sheathing. Always examine the wires for damage after removing the sheathing.

REFRESHER COURSE
Grounding NM cable

If the box is metal, code requires it to be grounded. The surest method is to connect both the device and the box to the ground wire using pigtails.

If the box is plastic, simply connect the ground wire to the device's grounding terminal.

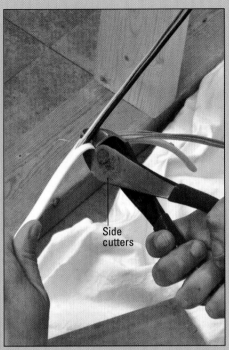

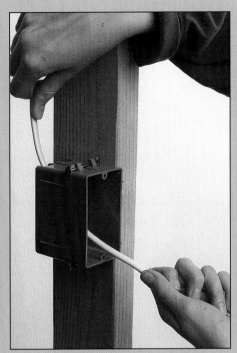

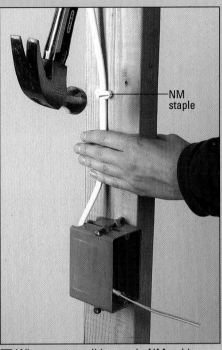

3 Pull back the plastic sheathing, as well as the paper that wraps the wires, exposing 6–8 inches of wire. Use a pair of side cutters to snip back the sheathing and paper. If you use a utility knife, cut away from the wires to avoid cutting or nicking the insulation.

4 Insert the wires into the box. With this type of plastic box, push the wires through a hole, which has a tab that grabs the cable. Check that about ½ inch of sheathing is visible inside the box. Other types of boxes use other clamping methods.

5 Wherever possible, staple NM cable firmly to a framing member, out of reach of nails. Cable should be stapled within 8 inches of the box and every 2–4 feet along the run of the cable. Check your local building codes.

Other clamping methods

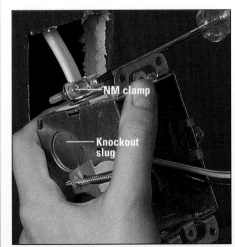

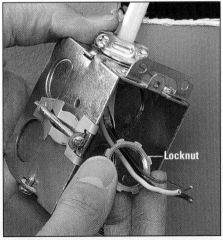

Clamp on box: Remove a knockout slug from a metal box and fasten an NM clamp in the hole. Insert the clamp and tighten the locknut. Insert the cable through the clamp; tighten the screws.

Cable first: Remove the locknut from the cable clamp and fasten the clamp to the cable. Then insert the cable with clamp body into the box, slide on the locknut, and tighten it.

Built-in clamps: Some boxes have built-in clamps. Slide in the cable and tighten the screws.

ARMORED CABLE

Some municipalities require either armored cable or conduit *(pages 38–41)*, rather than NM. Even if your local codes do not demand it, you may choose to install armored cable for added safety, especially wherever cable will be exposed.

Pluses and minuses
The coiled metal sheathing that wraps armored cable protects its wires from puncture by nails, unless a nail hits it dead-center. (Even conduit cannot offer absolute protection against a direct hit.) You may want to run armored cable behind moldings where it comes near nails *(pages 50–51)*. Armored cable costs more than NM, takes longer to strip and clamp, and can't make tight turns. With some practice, you can install armored cable nearly as quickly as NM.

    BX cable has no ground wire *(page 37, lower right)*, is common in older homes, and is still available in some areas. Local code may limit use of BX to no more than 6 feet; then ground wire must be used. **MC cable** has a green-insulated ground wire, used like the bare ground wire in NM cable.

1 Bend the cable about 10 inches from its end and squeeze with your hand until the coils of the armor come apart. If you can't do this by hand, use pliers or employ one of the other cutting methods shown *below.*

2 Firmly grip the cable on each side of the cut and twist until the split-apart armor coil pops out, away from the wires. Use two pairs of pliers if you can't do this by hand.

REFRESHER COURSE
Grounding MC cable

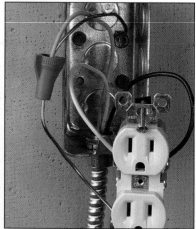

MC cable has a ground wire. Attach it the same way you would the ground wire in NM cable *(page 31)*, except that you'll have to strip the green insulation first.

Other cutting methods

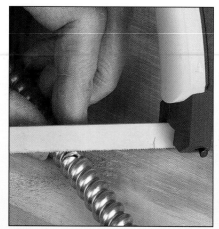

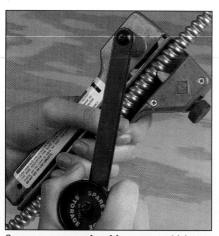

If the method shown in the steps above seems too difficult, try cutting the cable with a **hacksaw.** Cut through just one of the coils and no more, so you won't damage any wires. Then twist and pull off the waste piece.

Or use an **armored-cable cutter,** which cuts at just the right depth. Adjust it for the size of cable, slip in the cable, and turn the crank.

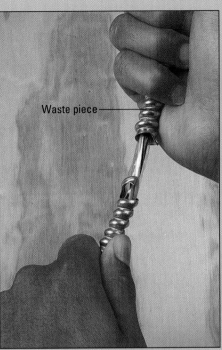

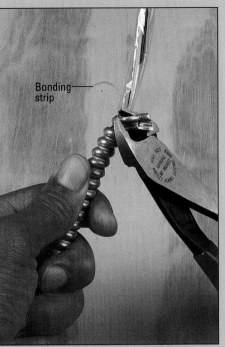

Bonding strip

3 Using side cutters, cut the exposed coil of sheathing. You may have to grab the coil with the side cutters and work it back and forth to open and make the cut.

4 If you are cutting a piece to length, slide back the sheathing and cut through the wires. Otherwise, slide the waste piece off and throw it away.

5 Cut off any sharp points of sheathing, using side cutters. Remove the paper wrapping and any thin plastic strips. If the cable is BX, it will have a thin metal bonding strip. Cut it to about 2 inches.

STANLEY PRO TIP: **Clamping armored cable**

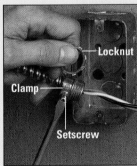

1 If the cable did not come with a bag of little bushings, purchase some. Slip a bushing over the wires and slide it down into the sheathing so it protects wires from the cut end of the armor.

2 Use an armored-cable clamp, which has a single setscrew. Remove the locknut and slide the clamp over the wires and down onto the bushing. Then tighten the setscrew.

3 Remove the knockout slug from the box. Guide the wires and the clamp through the hole. Slip the locknut over the wires and screw it onto the clamp. Tighten the nut by levering it with a screwdriver or tapping it with a screwdriver and hammer.

BX cable with a bonding strip

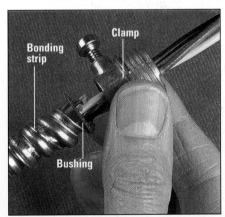

The metal sheathing of BX cable acts as the ground; a thin metal bonding strip helps ensure a conductive connection. Before putting on a cable clamp, wrap a strip 2 inches long around the sheathing.

METAL CONDUIT

Conduit offers superior protection and safety for wires. Even if local codes permit NM or armored cable in a basement, garage, attic, or crawlspace, consider installing conduit to protect wiring.

Choosing conduit

Metal conduit comes in several thicknesses. For most interior home installations, EMT (also called thinwall) is strong enough. Outdoors, use intermediate metal conduit (IMC), or PVC conduit *(page 40)*. PVC is sometimes used indoors as well.

Metal conduit may serve as the path for grounding, or local codes may require you to run a green-insulated ground wire. If you use PVC pipe, you definitely need a ground wire, either green-insulated or bare copper. **If there will be no ground wire, take extra care that all the connections in metal conduit are firm; one loose joint could break the grounding path.**

Conduit fittings

A conduit bender, used by professional electricians, is a fairly expensive tool that takes time to master. Unless you will be running lots of metal conduit, you'll save time by buying prebent fittings. A coupling joins two pieces of conduit end to end. A sweep makes a slow turn through which wires can slide easily. A pulling elbow makes a sharper turn.

The setscrew fittings shown here are commonly used with EMT conduit; they provide joints that are firm but not waterproof. For weather-tight joints, use IMC conduit and compression fittings *(page 103)*.

Flexible metal conduit

Flexible metal conduit, also called Greenfield, is like armored cable without the wires. It's not cheap, so it is typically used only in places where it would be difficult to run conduit.

When installing a hardwired appliance, such as an electric water heater or cooktop *(page 111)*, buy an electrical "whip," which is a section of armored cable equipped with the correct fittings for attaching to that specific appliance.

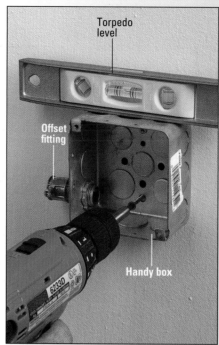

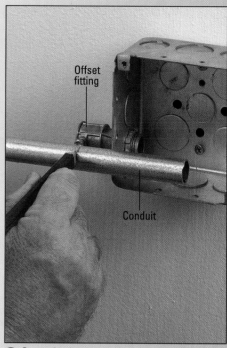

1 Anchor metal boxes to the wall with screws. For exposed wiring, use "handy boxes," which have rounded edges and metal covers. An offset fitting allows the conduit to run tight up against the wall.

2 Once the boxes are installed, measure the conduit for cutting. The surest method is to hold a piece in place and mark it, rather than using a tape measure. Remember that the conduit will slide about an inch into each fitting.

Metal conduit

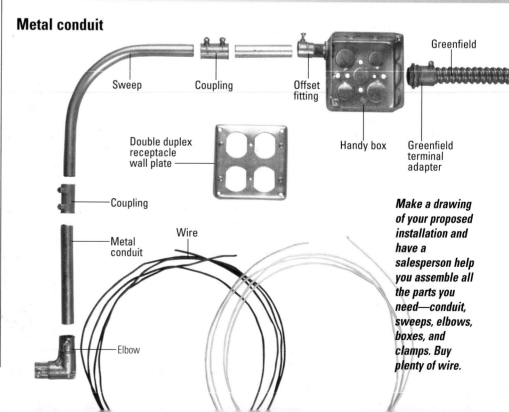

Sweep · Coupling · Offset fitting · Greenfield

Double duplex receptacle wall plate · Handy box · Greenfield terminal adapter

Coupling · Metal conduit · Wire · Elbow

Make a drawing of your proposed installation and have a salesperson help you assemble all the parts you need—conduit, sweeps, elbows, boxes, and clamps. Buy plenty of wire.

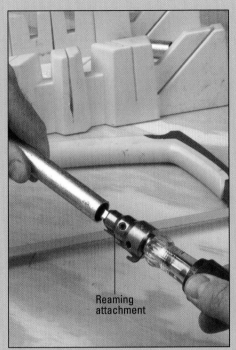

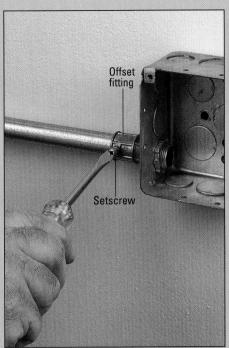

3 Cut the conduit to fit with a hacksaw. Do not use a tubing cutter, which creates sharp edges inside the conduit that could damage wire insulation. Remove the burrs inside and out. A conduit-reaming attachment on a screwdriver makes this easy.

4 Slide the conduit all the way into a fitting and tighten the setscrew. Test to make sure the connection is tight. (If you will not be installing a ground wire, these connections are critical for grounding.)

5 Anchor the conduit with a one- or two-hole strap at least every 6 feet and within 2 feet of each box. The larger the conduit, the closer the straps need to be. Check with local codes. Screws should be driven into joists or studs, not just into drywall.

Conduit that's large enough

Make sure the wires have ample room inside the conduit to slide through easily. Local codes have detailed regulations regarding conduit size, but in general, ½-inch conduit is large enough for five or fewer wires; ¾-inch conduit is used for more than five wires. When in doubt, or if you might run more wire in the future, buy the larger size—it doesn't cost much more.

Anchoring conduit

Anchor conduit with one- or two-hole straps every 6 feet and within 2 feet of each box.

A pulling elbow every fourth turn

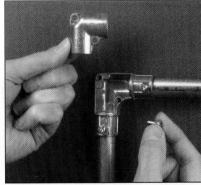

Every time you make a turn, it gets harder for the wires to slide through. If the conduit will make more than three turns before entering a box, install a pulling elbow so you can access the wires. Never make a splice here, just use it as an access point when pulling wires.

STANLEY PRO TIP: **Anchoring to masonry**

To attach boxes and straps to concrete, block, or brick, buy masonry screws and the correct masonry bit. Level the box and drill pilot holes.

Drive a masonry screw into the pilot hole, being careful not to overtighten it. The combination of proper hole and screw provides much more secure attachment than plastic anchors.

PVC CONDUIT

Plastic conduit is nearly as durable as metal conduit and it costs less. Some local codes permit it for exposed indoor wiring as well as for outdoor installations *(pages 100–107)*.

When installing PVC, connect four or five pieces in a dry run, then dismantle and glue the pieces together. When making a turn, take care that the elbow or sweep is facing in exactly the right direction when you glue it. Once the glue sets, there's no way to make adjustments. Work in a well-ventilated area when using PVC primer and cement; the fumes are powerful and dangerous.

Consult your local codes for the correct PVC cement. You may be required to apply purple-colored primer to every piece before you apply the cement. **Always run a green-insulated ground wire through PVC pipe.**

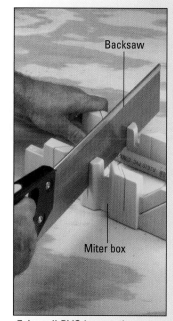

Backsaw

Miter box

1 Install PVC boxes, then measure and mark the conduit for a cut. Cut with a backsaw and miter box, or a hacksaw, or a circular saw equipped with a plywood blade.

Alignment mark

Primer

2 Use alignment marks to ensure that the pieces will face in the right direction. Apply PVC primer (if needed) and cement to the outside of the conduit and to the inside of the fitting.

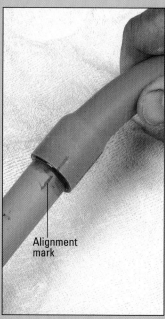

Alignment mark

3 Immediately push the conduit into the fitting, twisting slightly to align the marks. Hold the pieces together for about 10 seconds; wipe away excess cement.

Flexible nonmetallic conduit

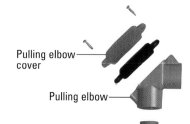

Pulling elbow cover

Pulling elbow

Coupling

PVC box

Handy box

Radius elbow

Terminal adapter

Have a salesperson help you assemble all the parts you need: conduit, couplings, elbows, sweeps, and PVC boxes. Connect to a metal box using a terminal adapter.

Flexible nonmetallic conduit

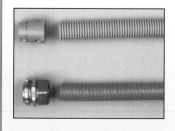

Flexible plastic tubing is a convenient way to channel wiring. Blue corrugated EMT tubing is used for indoor installations; moisture-impermeable tubing is used outdoors. Both come in long coils. Check to see whether these products are allowed by your local codes.

PULLING WIRES THROUGH CONDUIT

If wires travel less than 6 feet through conduit and make only one or two turns, you may be able to simply push them through. For longer runs, use a fish tape.

If wires become kinked while you work, they will get stuck. So have a helper feed the wire carefully from one end of the conduit while you pull at the other end. If you must work alone, precut the wires (leave yourself an extra 2 feet or so) and unroll them so that they can slide smoothly through the conduit.

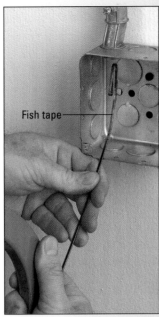

1 At a box or pulling elbow, push the fish tape into the conduit and thread it back to the point of entry.

2 Strip 6 inches of insulation from one wire, 8 inches from another wire, 10 inches from a third wire, and so on. Fold the wires over the fish tape as shown and wrap tightly with electrician's tape.

3 Pull smoothly, using long strokes to avoid stopping and starting. If the wires get stuck, back up a foot or so and start again.

TEAM UP TO PULL WIRE THROUGH CONDUIT

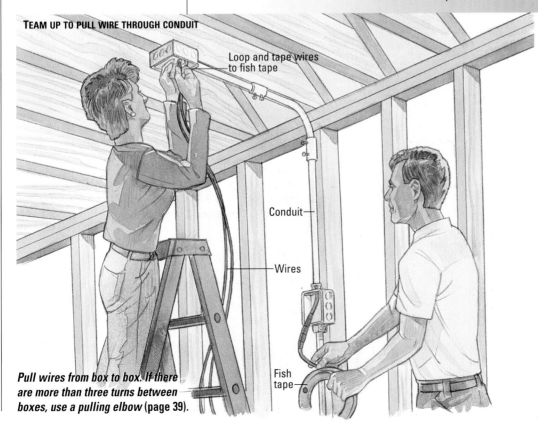

Loop and tape wires to fish tape

Conduit

Wires

Fish tape

Pull wires from box to box. If there are more than three turns between boxes, use a pulling elbow (page 39).

(page 39)

STANLEY PRO TIP

Pulling lubricant

If the pulling gets tough, try squirting some pulling lubricant on the wires. Don't use soap, detergent, oil, or grease, which can damage wire insulation.

GRABBING POWER

When planning new electrical service, begin by deciding where you can tap into power. If you are adding a couple of receptacles or lights, it is usually easiest to grab power from a nearby receptacle or junction box. First, however, make sure the new service will not overload the circuit (*pages 24–25*).

If nearby boxes are on circuits that do not have enough available wattage for the new service, try a box farther away. If no circuit is usable or if the new service needs its own circuit, run cable all the way to the service panel and connect to a new circuit breaker (*pages 112–113*).

If you need to run cable through walls and ceilings to get at power, see *pages 48–55*.

PRESTART CHECKLIST

☐ **TIME**
About two hours to connect new cable to an existing receptacle or junction box (not including cutting a pathway for the cable and patching walls)

☐ **TOOLS**
Voltage tester, drill, saw, hammer, close-work hacksaw, screwdriver, strippers, longnose pliers, lineman's pliers.

☐ **SKILLS**
Stripping wire and connecting wire to terminals, running cable through walls, prying and cutting nails

☐ **PREP**
Spread a drop cloth or towel on the floor. Run cable to the box from which you will grab power (*pages 45–53*).

☐ **MATERIALS**
New cable, wire nuts, electrician's tape, cable clamps, remodel box

1 To grab power from a receptacle, make a load list to verify that there is room on the circuit for new service. **Shut off power to the circuit and test that power is not present.** Disconnect the receptacle.

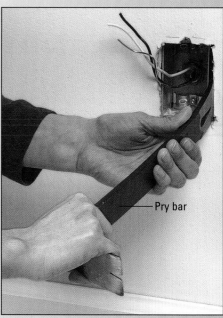

2 If the box is inside a wall, either cut a hole in the wall to get at the box or pull the box out. Pry with a flat pry bar, then remove the nails or cut through them with a close-work hacksaw.

Grabbing power from a junction box and switch

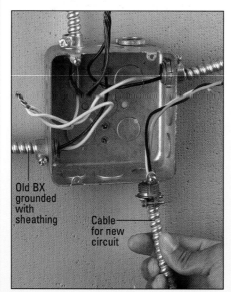

To grab power from a junction box, **shut off power,** remove wire nuts, and splice the new wires. You may need to cover the resulting splice with larger wire nuts.

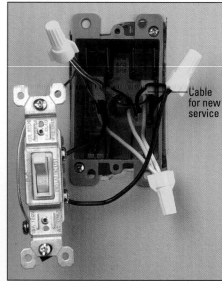

You can grab power from a switch box only if power enters the box (rather than going to the fixture) and two cables are present. Connect with pigtails as shown.

Remodel box

3 Pull out the box carefully—the cable may be stapled to a stud. Disconnect the cable(s) from the old box. Choose a remodel box to fit the hole *(pages 12–13)*. Clamp the old and new cables to the remodel box.

4 Push the remodel box back into place and clamp it to the wall.

5 If the new receptacle is at the end of the run (with only one cable entering the box), simply connect the new wires to the proper terminals and connect the grounds.

STANLEY PRO TIP

Wire into the old box

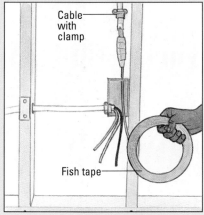

Cable with clamp

Fish tape

You may be able to avoid the step of removing the old box. Pry out a knockout slug and run a fish tape up through the hole. Attach the tape to cable that has been stripped and has a clamp attached (with the locknut removed). Pull the wires through, seat the clamp, and screw on the locknut.

WHAT IF...
You grab power from a mid-run receptacle?

If two cables enter the box, the receptacle is in the middle of a run. Splice the wires and connect to terminals with pigtails, as shown. The purpose of pigtails is to avoid multiple connections to one terminal screw where they could easily short or come loose. Make pigtails by removing the sheathing from about 8 inches of NM cable. Strip about ½ inch for each end of the black and white wires and attach them as shown.

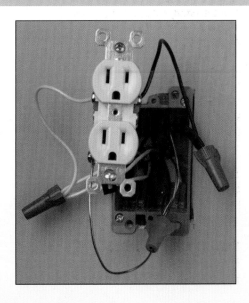

Code issues: Cable must be clamped to the box or stapled to a stud within 8 inches of the box. NM cable is the easiest to run, but some localities require armored cable or conduit. Some localities require metal rather than plastic boxes.

INSTALLING BOXES IN FRAMING

Installing new wiring is much easier if the framing in a room is uncovered than if the walls and ceilings are covered with drywall or plaster *(pages 48–55)*.

Buy switch and receptacle boxes that meet local codes *(pages 22–23)* and that are large enough for the wires they will hold *(page 13)*. It's easy to underestimate so buy extra supplies. At the same time you install boxes, attach fans, lights, or other fixtures that need to be hardwired.

Local codes specify where cable should run and at what height to place receptacle and switch boxes. Check codes before you begin.

PRESTART CHECKLIST

☐ **TIME**
About an hour to install eight wall or ceiling boxes

☐ **TOOLS**
Hammer, tape measure, drill, screwdriver

☐ **SKILLS**
Measuring, driving nails

☐ **PREP**
Remove all wall surfaces and obstructions in the room. Make and follow a written plan that plots the location of each box.

☐ **MATERIALS**
New-work electrical boxes, 1¼-inch wood screws (not drywall screws)

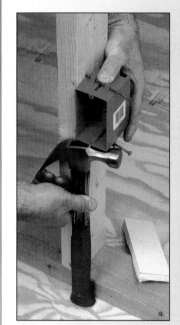

1 Receptacle boxes are typically placed 12 inches up from the floor. Measure with a tape measure, or set your hammer upright on the floor, and rest the box on top of the handle.

Drywall scrap

2 The front edge of the box must be flush with the finished wall surface, usually ½-inch-thick drywall. Some boxes have depth gauges. Or use a scrap of drywall to position the box.

3 Drive the box's nails into the stud or joist. If the box attaches with a flange, drive screws or nails to anchor the box (below).

Using a mud ring

Adapter rings, also called mud rings, are typically ½ inch or ⅝ inch thick. Choose a ring that matches the thickness of the drywall or paneling you will install. Attach the box flush with the front edge of the framing member, then add the ring.

STANLEY PRO TIP

Mounting a ceiling light fixture box

Decide where you want a ceiling light fixture to go (usually the center of a room). Attach a flanged box directly to a ceiling joist (left). For more precise placement, install a box attached to a hanger bar; the box slides along the bar. Note: A hanger bar cannot support a ceiling fan; you must use a fan-rated box *(page 12)*.

RUNNING CABLE IN FRAMING

Nonmetallic cable is acceptable under most building codes, but some localities require armored cable or conduit. Armored cable is run much like the NM cable shown, though you may need to drill larger holes and you'll have more difficulty turning corners. To run conduit through framing, use a level or a chalk line to make sure the holes are aligned for straight runs.

If a wayward nail pierces NM cable, the result could be disastrous. Place holes in the framing out of reach of drywall nails and attach protective plates at every hole.

PRESTART CHECKLIST

☐ **TIME**
About three hours to run cable and attach to seven or eight wall or ceiling boxes

☐ **TOOLS**
Drill, ¾-inch spade bits, screwdriver, strippers, lineman's pliers, hammer, tape measure, level

☐ **SKILLS**
Drilling, stripping cable sheathing and wire insulation, attaching staples

☐ **PREP**
Double-check that all the boxes are correctly positioned; clear the room of all obstructions

☐ **MATERIALS**
Correct cable (page 11), staples appropriate to cable type, protective nail plates

1 Use a tape measure and level to mark holes that will line up in a straight line about 12 inches above the boxes. With a sharp spade bit, drill a ¾-inch hole through the center of each stud.

2 Uncoil cable carefully from the box to prevent kinks. Pull the cable through the holes. The cable should be fairly straight but should not be taut.

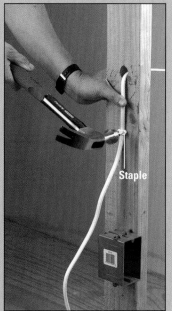
3 Within 8 inches of a plastic box or 12 inches of a metal box, anchor the cable in the middle of the stud with a staple. Drive staples every 2 feet where cable runs along a framing member.

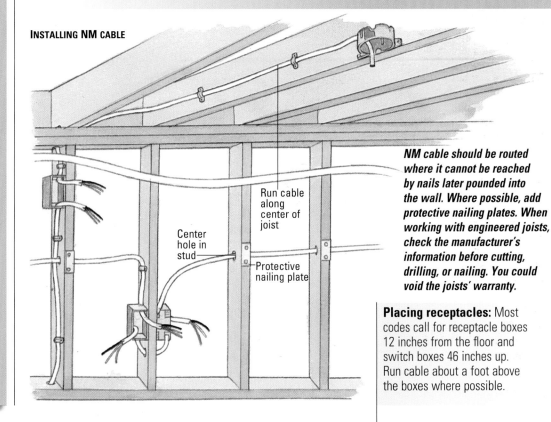
INSTALLING NM CABLE

Run cable along center of joist • Center hole in stud • Protective nailing plate

NM cable should be routed where it cannot be reached by nails later pounded into the wall. Where possible, add protective nailing plates. When working with engineered joists, check the manufacturer's information before cutting, drilling, or nailing. You could void the joists' warranty.

Placing receptacles: Most codes call for receptacle boxes 12 inches from the floor and switch boxes 46 inches up. Run cable about a foot above the boxes where possible.

Running cable in framing *(continued)*

4 Mark where you will strip sheathing and cut the cable. About ½ inch of sheathing should enter the box, and the wires inside the box should be 8 to 12 inches long (you can always trim them later).

5 With a hammer and screwdriver, open the knockout. On some plastic boxes you remove the knockout entirely. For the one shown, crack open one end of the tab so it can grab the cable. A metal box may have a built-in clamp, or you may have to add a clamp before sliding in the cable.

6 Wherever a nail might accidentally pierce the cable, attach a protective nailing plate. Tap the plate in place and hammer it in. Attach a plate on both sides of the stud, if needed.

Protective nailing plate

STANLEY PRO TIP: **Turning a corner**

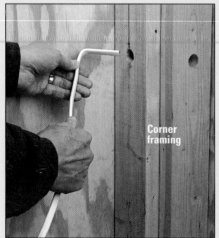

Corner framing

Lineman's pliers

1 When you reach a corner, drill a hole in each stud. Bend the cable into an L shape.

2 Poke the cable through the first hole and wiggle it into the next hole. When the cable starts to stick out the second hole, grab it with pliers and pull.

WHAT IF...
You have a lot of holes to drill?

A standard ⅜-inch drill may overheat after drilling four or five holes. If you have many holes to bore, rent a ½-inch right-angle drill. When using it, hold on tightly and brace yourself; it has more power and can twist around, possibly causing an injury.

WORKING WITH METAL STUDS

Contractors have been using metal studs for decades. More and more homeowners are discovering that these save money and are easy to install.

Metal studs have precut holes designed to accommodate electrical and plumbing lines. When running NM cable through metal framing, inspect the holes to be sure that there are no rough or sharp edges that could damage insulation. Always use the special bushings (Step 2) designed to protect wiring.

PRESTART CHECKLIST

☐ **TIME**
About three hours to run cable and attach to seven or eight wall or ceiling boxes

☐ **TOOLS**
Screwdriver, tin snips, strippers, variable-speed drill, lineman's pliers, nonconducting ladder

☐ **SKILLS**
Installing metal framing, stripping cable sheathing and wire insulation, attaching bushings

☐ **PREP**
Assemble metal framing and clear the room of obstructions

☐ **MATERIALS**
Bushings, cable, boxes designed for metal studs

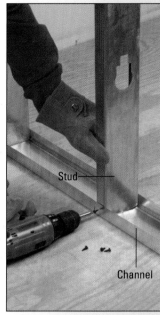

Stud

Channel

1 Cut metal studs and channels with tin snips. Slide the studs into channels at the bottom and top of the wall and anchor each joint by driving a self-piercing screw.

Bushing

2 Where the cable will run through a stud, snap a protective bushing into place. These come in two pieces that press together.

3 Pull cable through as you would through holes in wood framing, sliding it through the protective bushings.

INSTALLING WIRING IN STEEL STUD FRAMING

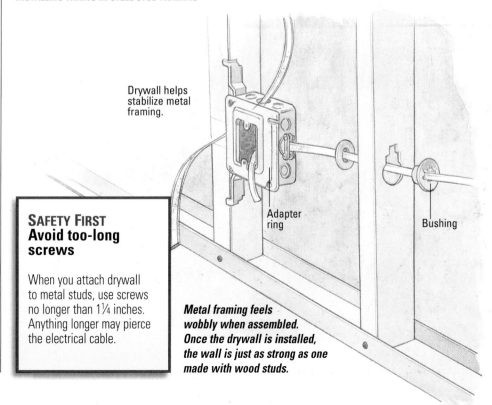

Drywall helps stabilize metal framing.

Adapter ring

Bushing

SAFETY FIRST
Avoid too-long screws

When you attach drywall to metal studs, use screws no longer than 1¼ inches. Anything longer may pierce the electrical cable.

Metal framing feels wobbly when assembled. Once the drywall is installed, the wall is just as strong as one made with wood studs.

INSTALLING BOXES IN FINISHED WALLS

Running cable through walls that are covered with drywall or plaster is probably the most difficult wiring task you will encounter. Plan the job carefully before starting; see *page 50* for the order of work.

Special remodel boxes (also called "cut-in" or "old-work" boxes) clamp themselves to the drywall or plaster rather than attaching to a framing member, making the work easier. However they will be only as strong as the wall surface to which they are clamped. If the drywall or plaster is damaged, cut a larger hole and install a box that attaches directly to a stud or joist. Select boxes that meet local codes *(pages 12–13)*. For a ceiling fan or a heavy light fixture, buy a fixture box that attaches to a fan-rated brace.

Before cutting a hole, use a stud finder to make sure no joist or stud is in the way.

PRESTART CHECKLIST

☐ **TIME**
About 15 minutes to cut a hole and install a remodel box (not including cutting a pathway for the cable and patching walls)

☐ **TOOLS**
Stud finder, torpedo level, utility knife, screwdriver, hammer, drill, drywall saw (or rotary cutter or saber saw)

☐ **SKILLS**
Measuring and cutting drywall

☐ **PREP**
Carefully plan the routes for the cables and the locations for the boxes *(pages 50–53)*. Spread a drop cloth or large towel on the floor below them.

☐ **MATERIALS**
Remodel boxes acceptable under local code, cable clamps if needed

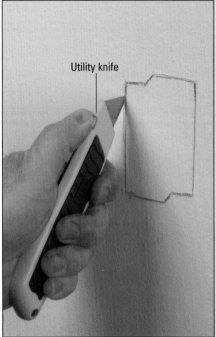

Utility knife

1 If the box does not come with a cardboard template, hold its face against the wall, use a torpedo level to make sure it is straight, and trace it. With a utility knife, cut the line deep enough to cut through the drywall paper.

Drywall saw

2 Cut the hole with a drywall saw. Cut to the inside of the knife cut to prevent fraying the paper. Test to make sure the box will fit in the hole.

WHAT IF...
The wall is made of plaster and lath?

Take your time cutting a lath-and-plaster wall—it's easy to damage the surrounding area. Most plaster is attached to ⅜-inch-thick wood lath, which cuts fairly easily if it does not vibrate. If it does vibrate as you saw, sections of plaster can loosen from the lath. It is difficult to make a neat hole in plaster and lath, so have patching plaster on hand. If plaster is attached to metal lath, cut all the way through the plaster with a knife and then cut the metal lath with side cutters.

Make several passes with a sharp knife. Drill starter holes at each corner and then cut with a saber saw. Press the saw firmly against the wall to minimize lath vibration.

Or use a rotary cutter equipped with a plaster-cutting blade. Practice first because this tool is hard to control.

Remodel box

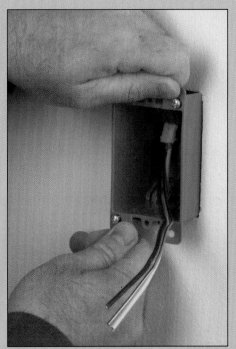

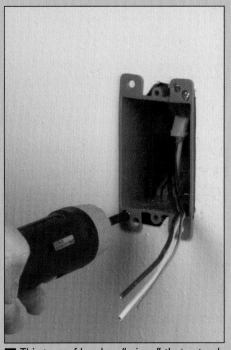

3 Run cable through the hole *(pages 50–53)*. Strip 12 inches of sheathing and run the cable into the box. Whichever clamping method the box uses, make sure ½ inch of sheathing shows inside the box and tug to make sure the cable is clamped tight.

4 Push the box into the hole. If it fits tightly, do not force it or you may damage the drywall. If needed, use a utility knife to enlarge the hole.

5 This type of box has "wings" that extend outward when you start to drive the screw and then grasp the back of the drywall as the screw is tightened (see below). Tighten the screw until you feel resistance and the box is firmly attached.

STANLEY PRO TIP

The old-fashioned way

To install a box in a lath-and-plaster wall, cut the hole and then remove ¾ inch of plaster above and below the hole. Loosen the setscrews and adjust the depth of the box's plaster ears so the box will be flush with the wall surface. Insert the box, drill pilot holes (lath cracks easily), and drive screws through the ears into the lath.

Other remodel-box options

The round plastic ceiling box (left) has "wings" that rotate out and behind the wall surface. One metal box (center) has a flange that springs outward when the box is inserted; tightening a screw brings the flange forward. A variation on this has side clamps that move out and toward the front as screws are tightened. Yet another type (right) uses separate mounting brackets that slide in after the box is inserted and bend over the sides of the box to lock it in place.

RUNNING CABLE THROUGH FINISHED ROOMS

When running new electrical service through rooms that are finished with drywall or plaster, plan carefully to minimize damage to walls and ceilings. Sometimes you can go through a basement or attic to get at the finished wall or ceiling. Or you may choose to remove a large section of drywall, which often means less work than repairing many smaller holes.

Begin by making a drawing of the room that includes the locations of all studs and joists. Use a stud finder to locate them. Plan the easiest—not necessarily the shortest—routes for cables. Also determine where the boxes will go. Sometimes moving a box over a few inches makes the run easier.

Once you have a plan, cut the holes for the remodel boxes *(pages 48–49)*, run the cable, and install the boxes. Connect the cable to a power source *(pages 42–43)*.

PRESTART CHECKLIST

☐ **TIME**
About half a day to run cable through a wall and a ceiling

☐ **TOOLS**
Stud finder, fish tapes, strippers, screwdriver, hammer, drill, fishing drill bit, pry bar, drywall saw or saber saw

☐ **SKILLS**
Measuring, cutting through drywall or plaster, using fish tapes

☐ **PREP**
Spread a drop cloth on the floor of the room and cut holes for the remodel boxes *(pages 48–49)*

☐ **MATERIALS**
Electrical cable, protective nail plates, electrician's tape

Behind base molding

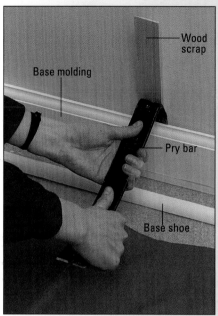

1 Pry away the base shoe (if any) and the base molding. Use a flat pry bar; place a scrap of wood under the bar to avoid damaging the wall.

2 Cut out a strip of drywall or plaster to reveal the bottom plate and studs. If possible, cut low enough so you can replace the base molding to cover your work. If the molding is less than 3 inches wide, see the tip on *page 51*.

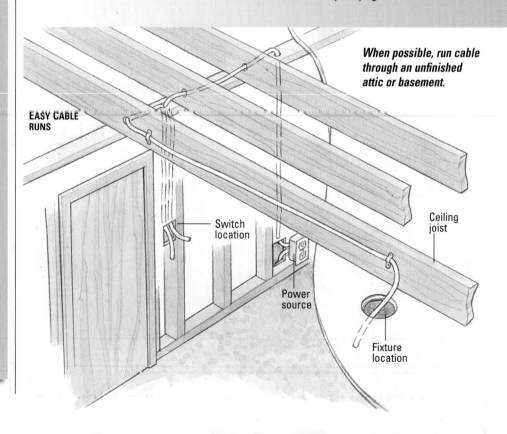

When possible, run cable through an unfinished attic or basement.

EASY CABLE RUNS

Switch location

Power source

Fixture location

Ceiling joist

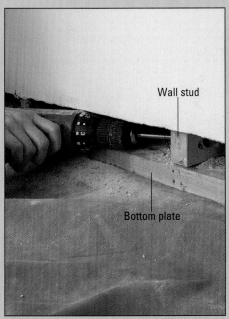

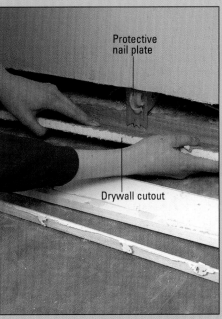

3 Drill ¾-inch holes near the bottom of studs. You may hit a nail or two with the drill bit, so have extra drill bits on hand to replace broken or dull ones.

4 Thread cable through the holes and pull it fairly tight. Once the cable is run, install a nail plate to protect each hole.

5 Replace the drywall and the molding. (If the wall is plaster, shim out the bottom plate so the molding can sit flat.) You may need to attach the drywall with adhesive and reposition some nails to avoid hitting the protective plates.

Run cable behind a door casing

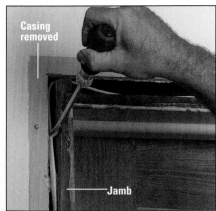

1 Pry off the casing. Where there is a gap between the jamb and framing, thread the cable. Where the jamb is tight against a stud, drill a hole so you can run cable through the wall. Door frames are attached to a double stud so the hole will be 3 inches long.

2 Install a protective plate wherever cable is at risk of being pierced by a nail. Use a chisel to cut a notch for the plate in the jamb so the casing sits snug up against the jamb.

STANLEY PRO TIP

Base cap when the base is not wide enough

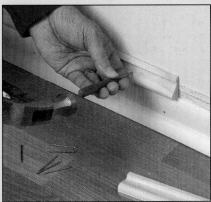

If you need to cut a hole too high for the base molding to cover, either replace the old molding with a wider base or install a base cap to add width to the base molding.

Through a basement

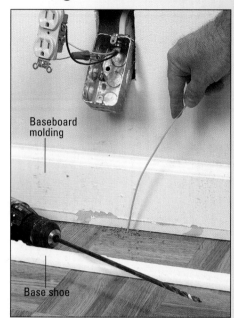

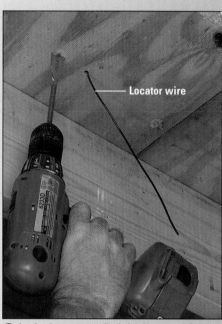

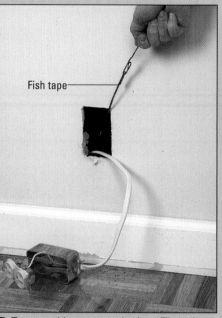

1 If the basement below is unfinished, remove the base shoe and drill a locator hole. Poke a wire down through the hole.

2 In the basement, find the locator wire. Drill a hole up through the middle of the bottom plate.

3 To run cable, remove the box. Thread one fish tape down through the knockout while a helper threads another fish tape up through the basement hole. Hook the tapes and pull up. If the box is difficult to remove, punch out a knockout slug and pull the cable through the hole in the box.

STANLEY PRO TIP: **Fishing into the attic**

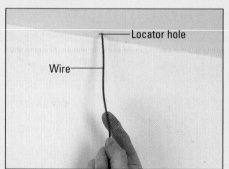

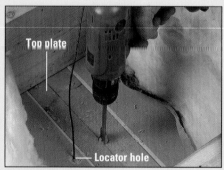

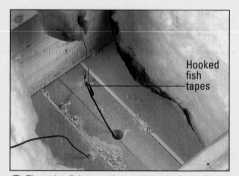

1 Drill a locator hole directly above the hole or box in the wall. Poke a wire through the hole. The wire may have to push through fiberglass or loose-fill insulation.

2 Near the locator hole, drill a ¾-inch hole through the center of the top plate. If your house has fire blocking (page 53), cut a hole in the wall and drill a hole through the blocking.

3 Thread a fish tape down through the attic hole while a helper threads a fish tape up through a box or hole in the wall. Once the tapes hook together, pull up.

Code variations
Your building department may forbid running cable around a door frame or may require armored cable in finished walls and ceilings.

Through walls and ceilings

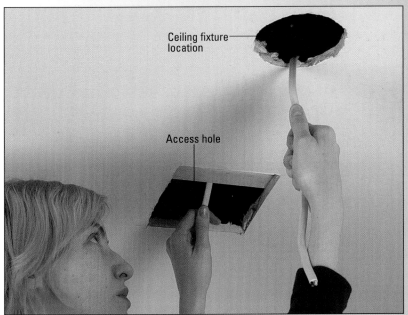

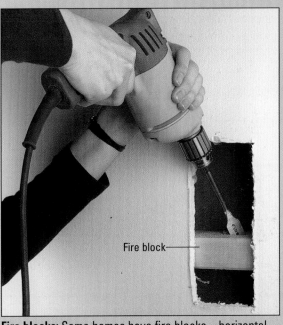

Middle of ceiling: If you need to run cable across the middle of a ceiling or wall, find the joists or studs and cut holes that are large enough for your hand to fit into. (Save drywall pieces and use them to patch the holes later.) Drill holes and thread the cable through. Once the cable is run, install protective nail plates.

Fire blocks: Some homes have fire blocks—horizontal 2×4s between the studs, usually 4 or 5 feet above the floor. Use a stud finder to locate one. Cut a hole in the wall and drill a hole through the fire block.

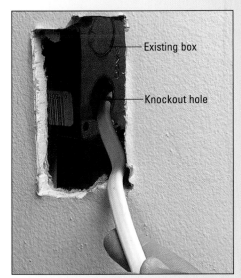

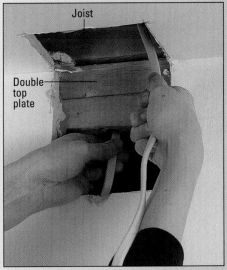

Using a fishing drill bit

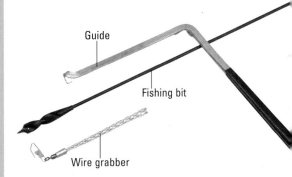

Behind a box: If the hole for a new box is behind an existing box, punch out a knockout slug in the existing box. Run fish tapes from both directions, hook them together, and pull through the box. Now you can pull cable through the box to the hole.

No attic access: To run cable up the wall and across the ceiling, cut holes in the wall and the ceiling. Drill a hole up through the top plate. If there is a joist in the way, drill a hole through it as well. Bend the cable and thread it through the holes.

A fishing bit reduces the number of holes in walls and ceilings. Drill a hole through the next joist or stud, using the guide to aim the bit. Fasten a wire to the bit and pull it back through the hole.

PATCHING WALLS

However painstakingly you plan cable runs, chances are you will have to repair walls and ceilings after the wiring work is finished. Cut holes in drywall as neatly as possible and save the cutouts so you can use them as patches later.

Allow plenty of time for patching. After applying the first coat of joint compound, you must let it dry, scrape and/or sand it, then apply second, third, and maybe even fourth coats before achieving a smooth surface.

Dry-mix joint compound, which is strong but hard to sand, comes in bags labeled "90," "45," or "20." The numbers indicate roughly how many minutes before the product hardens. Ready-mix joint compound, which comes in buckets, is easier to apply and sand but is not as strong. A good plan is to apply dry-mix compound for the first coat and use ready-mix for subsequent coats.

PRESTART CHECKLIST

☐ **TIME**
About an hour to install a patch and apply the first coat of compound; several 15-minute sessions on following days, to sand and apply additional coats

☐ **TOOLS**
Drywall saw, utility knife, hammer, putty knife, drill, 8- and 12-inch taping blades, corner trowel, drywall-sanding block with 80- and 100-grit sandpapers or screens

☐ **SKILLS**
Cutting drywall, applying joint compound, painting

☐ **PREP**
Make sure the wiring is correct and have it inspected if required before you cover it up. Spread a drop cloth on the floor below.

☐ **MATERIALS**
Drywall screws, drywall for patching, 1×4 scraps, mesh tape, joint compound

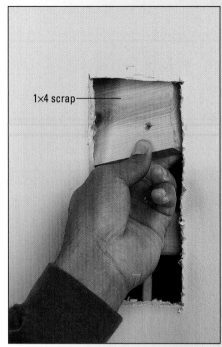

1 Where there is no framing member to attach the drywall to, slip a 1×4 or backer piece behind the hole so that half its width is behind the wall surface and half is visible.

2 Hold the backer piece tight against the back of the drywall and drive 1¼-inch drywall screws through the drywall and into the backer piece. Drive each screw until the backer piece is drawn tight to the drywall.

Patching plaster walls

1 Pry or chip away any loose plaster around the damaged area. If the whole wall has loose plaster, call in a professional plasterer.

2 Buy drywall that's no thicker than the plaster. Cut a piece to fit the hole and attach it to the lath with screws.

3 Fill the gaps between the patch and the wall with joint compound. Apply tape and joint compound as described above.

Original cutout as patch

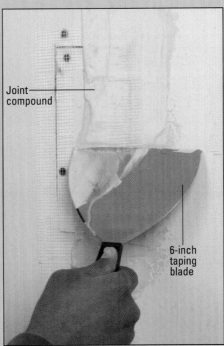

Joint compound

6-inch taping blade

Screen sander

3 Use the original drywall cutout or cut a new piece to fit. Cut off any dangling scraps of paper. Attach the patch with drywall screws. Screw heads must sink below the surface of the drywall without tearing the paper.

4 Cut and apply pieces of self-sticking fiberglass mesh tape. With a taping blade, apply enough joint compound to cover the tape. Smooth the compound.

5 When the first coat dries, scrape away high spots and apply a second coat, feathering out the edges a bit farther. When it dries, sand it. Apply and sand as many coats as needed to achieve a surface that looks and feels smooth. Prime and paint.

Patching at a corner

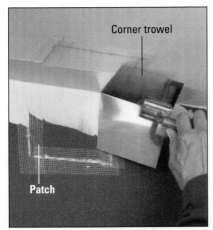

Corner trowel

Patch

A smooth surface in a corner is difficult to achieve. Use a corner trowel to form a perfect inside corner when applying the first coat. Use a straight trowel to smooth the wall and ceiling during subsequent coats.

STANLEY PRO TIP

Blending with textured surface

A textured wall surface may have been applied with a special tool. Patterns vary from one applicator to another. Try this trick: Make the cutout carefully, then replace it and caulk rather than tape the joints. To mimic a texture, practice on scraps of drywall, experimenting with various tools. (Sometimes it helps to add a handful of sand to a gallon of joint compound.) If a ceiling has a blown-on "popcorn" or "cottage cheese" surface, buy special patching compound, which can be sprayed on or applied with a trowel.

Need a small piece of drywall?

Most home centers sell broken pieces of drywall at a fraction of their original price.

Cover it beautifully

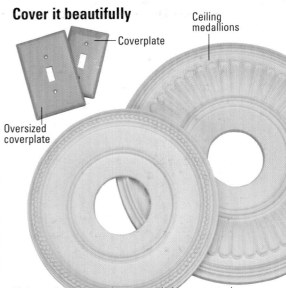

Coverplate

Ceiling medallions

Oversized coverplate

If the wall is damaged near a switch or receptacle, an oversized coverplate may cover the blemish and save patching work. To cover a damaged ceiling near a light fixture, install a medallion, which can be painted to match the ceiling.

CONNECTING LIGHTS & OUTLETS

Any wiring project should begin with a detailed plan. The chapter entitled "Planning New Electrical Service" will help you prepare a thorough, easy-to-read description. Make sure existing or new circuits can handle the new installation *(page 24)*. Present your plans to the local building department and receive a permit before beginning work.

Getting ready
Your inspector may approve NM cable, or you might have to install conduit or armored cable. Metal boxes may be required; plastic may be allowed. Determine how ground wires should be connected *(page 22)* and how cable should be clamped to the boxes *(page 14)*.

Most projects call for two-wire cable, but some require three-wire cable or even four wires running in conduit or Greenfield. Buy plenty of cable; it's easy to underestimate how much you'll need.

Unless you face special circumstances, use #12 wire for 20-amp circuits and #14 wire for 15-amp circuits. If your existing service uses armored cable or conduit, you can usually switch to NM cable if the cable runs into a box and the ground wire is connected according to code.

Test all new receptacles with a receptacle analyzer *(page 8)*. It tells you instantly whether the receptacle is properly grounded and polarized.

Some building departments require that lights be on dedicated lighting circuits, rather than sharing a circuit with receptacles. Other departments allow circuits to combine the two.

Planning a remodeling project
If a wiring project is part of a larger job, plan the order of work so different tasks and contractors do not collide. The first order of business is removing wall surfaces and any framing. Then comes rough plumbing, then rough electrical—installing boxes and running cable. If you install receptacles and switches at this point, protect them with tape. Better yet, wait until after the walls and ceilings are drywalled (with openings cut) and painted to install receptacles, switches, and fixtures.

Make your home more convenient and appealing by adding new receptacles and light fixtures.

CHAPTER PREVIEW

Adding new receptacles
page 58

240-volt receptacles
page 60

Two circuit receptacles
page 62

Split receptacles
page 63

Switched receptacles
page 64

New light fixtures add style and illumination. Bathrooms are often prime candidates for new fixtures, especially when power can be grabbed from an overhead switched fixture.

Cable for wall-mounted fixtures can be run from below (through a basement or crawlspace) or from above (through an attic) to minimize damage to the ceiling and wall.

Switched fixtures
page 66

Three-way switches
page 70

Undercabinet fluorescents
page 74

Recessed cans
page 76

Wall-mounted lighting
page 80

ADDING A NEW RECEPTACLE

The following steps show how to tap into an existing receptacle to grab power for a new receptacle. If doing this will cause the circuit to overload *(pages 24–25)* or if there is no conveniently located receptacle, consider grabbing power from a junction box in the basement or from a nearby light fixture or switch *(pages 42–43)*.

If one or more new receptacles will supply heavy power users, run cable all the way to the service panel and install a new circuit *(pages 112–113)*.

When connecting to a 15-amp circuit, install a standard receptacle and #14 wire. When connecting to a 20-amp circuit, use #12 wire and a special 20-amp receptacle.

PRESTART CHECKLIST

☐ **TIME**
About two hours to run cable and make connections (not including cutting a pathway for the cable and patching the walls)

☐ **TOOLS**
Voltage tester, drill, saw, hammer, fish tape, screwdriver, strippers, longnose pliers, lineman's pliers, utility knife, stud finder, torpedo level, tape measure, pry bar, perhaps a drywall saw or saber saw

☐ **SKILLS**
Stripping and connecting wires to terminals, installing boxes, running cable through walls and ceilings

☐ **PREP**
Lay a drop cloth on the floor below

☐ **MATERIALS**
New receptacle, cable, remodel box and clamps, wire nuts, electrician's tape, protective nail plates, cable staples

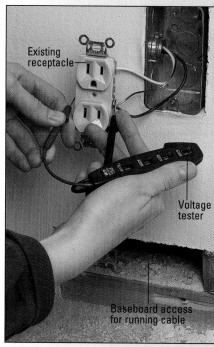

Existing receptacle

Voltage tester

Baseboard access for running cable

1 **Shut off power to the circuit.** Cut and drill a pathway for the cable *(pages 45–53)*. Pull out the receptacle from which you will be grabbing power and test to make sure power is not present *(page 7)*. Move the receptacle to the side or disconnect and remove it.

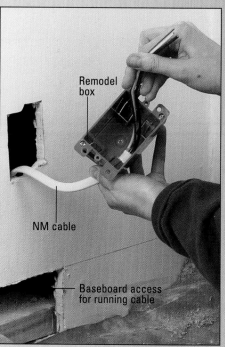

Remodel box

NM cable

Baseboard access for running cable

2 Cut a hole for a remodel box. Run cable from the area near the existing box to the hole, clamp the cable to the box, and install the new box *(pages 48–49)*.

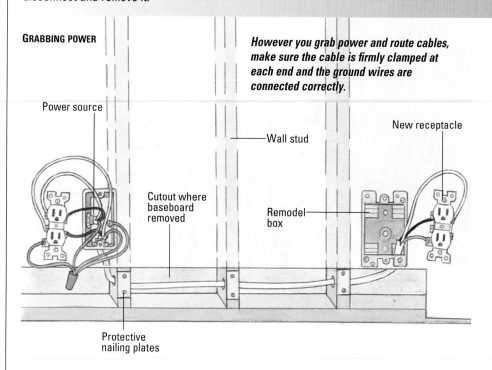

GRABBING POWER

However you grab power and route cables, make sure the cable is firmly clamped at each end and the ground wires are connected correctly.

Power source

Wall stud

New receptacle

Cutout where baseboard removed

Remodel box

Protective nailing plates

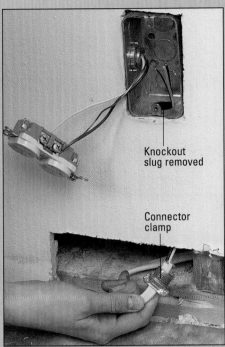

Wrap tape around receptacle before pushing into box

Knockout slug removed

Locknut tightened

Connector clamp

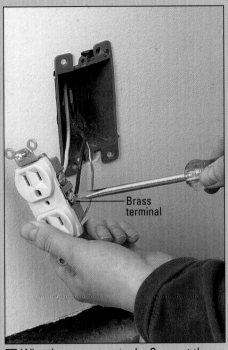

Brass terminal

3 Pry up a knockout slug in the old box and twist it out with pliers. (If you can't do this, remove the box and replace it with a remodel box.) Remove the sheathing from the cable, strip the wires, and attach a connector clamp to the cable. Push the cable into the box and fasten the clamp.

4 Strip and run cable into the existing box and tighten the clamp. Connect the new wires to existing wiring. Attach the ground wires, using a pigtail. Connect the white wire to the available silver terminal and the black wire to the brass terminal.

5 Wire the new receptacle. Connect the ground wire to the ground screw, the white wire to the silver terminal, and the black wire to the brass terminal.

REFRESHER COURSE
Wiring a GFCI

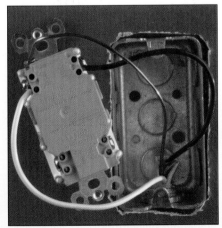

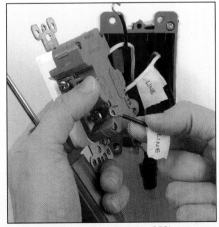

To wire a ground fault circuit interrupter (GFCI) at the end of the run, connect wires to the LINE terminals as marked on the back of the device.

To protect receptacles after the GFCI, connect wires supplying power to LINE terminals; wires leading to other receptacles are connected to LOAD terminals.

EXISTING WIRING
Wiring a middle-of-run receptacle

Pigtail

If the existing receptacle box has two cables and there are no available terminals on the receptacle, disconnect all the wires. Hook up pigtails and connect the pigtails to the terminals.

ADDING A 240-VOLT RECEPTACLE

Electric water heaters, dryers, ranges, and other major appliances use 240 volts—twice the voltage of most fixtures. Each appliance needs a separate double-pole breaker. (See *pages 112–113* for how to install a new breaker.)

Various 240-volt receptacles are made for specific amperages and types of appliance. Make sure your appliance will be able to plug in. Some receptacles deliver not only 240 volts, but also 120 volts to power lights and timers. In some cases, older receptacles use only three wires. But newer codes call for four wires—black and red hot wires, a white neutral wire, and a green or bare ground wire. Use #12 wire for 20-amp service, #10 wire for 30 amps, #8 wire for 40 amps, and #6 wire for 50 amps. Check local codes for what conduit, Greenfield, or cable to use.

Work with extreme caution: 240 volts can cause serious bodily harm.

PRESTART CHECKLIST

☐ **TIME**
About three hours to run cable (not including cutting and patching walls) and connect a breaker and receptacle

☐ **TOOLS**
Voltage tester, drill, saw, hammer, nonconductive ladder, flashlight, fish tape, screwdriver, strippers, longnose pliers, lineman's pliers

☐ **SKILLS**
Stripping and connecting wires, installing boxes, running cable

☐ **PREP**
Lay a towel or drop cloth below where you will cut into walls. Cut a pathway.

☐ **MATERIALS**
240-volt (or 120/240-volt) receptacle, wire of correct size, Greenfield, conduit or NM cable (if allowed), wire nuts, clamps, double-pole circuit breaker

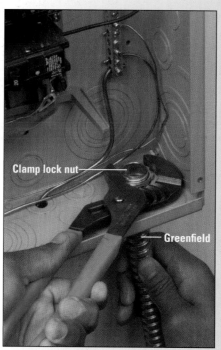

Clamp lock nut
Greenfield

1 Choose conduit or Greenfield large enough so the wires can slide easily. Remove a knockout slug from the service panel (make sure it's the right size) and clamp the conduit or Greenfield to the panel.

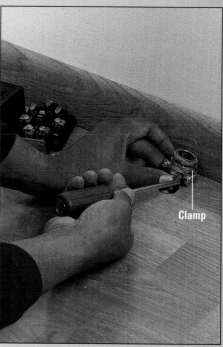

Clamp

2 Run the conduit or Greenfield from the service panel to the receptacle location *(pages 38–40, 50–53)* and attach a clamp. You may need to drill one-inch holes. The receptacle may be mounted on the floor or in a wall box.

Air-conditioner receptacle

White wire marked black

1 A large-capacity window air-conditioner calls for a 20-amp, 240-volt receptacle. Route 12/2 cable from the service panel to a receptacle box *(pages 42–53)*. Connect the grounds. Mark the white wire black. Connect the white and black wires to the terminals.

2 At the service panel, **shut off the main breaker.** Make room for a double-pole breaker. Connect the ground wire to the grounding bar and the black and white wires to the breaker. Snap in the breaker.

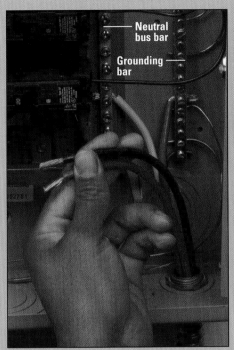

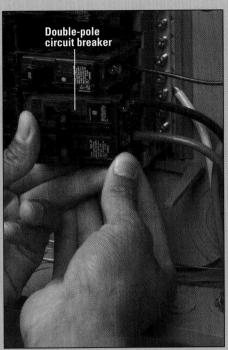

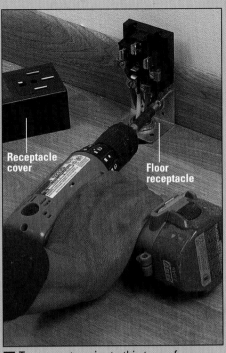

3 **Shut off the main breaker.** Fish wires *(page 41)* from the receptacle location to the panel. Attach the white wire to the neutral bus bar and the ground wire to the grounding bar.

4 Connect the red and black wires to the breaker terminals. Snap the breaker into place. (See *pages 112–113* for more detailed instructions.)

5 To connect a wire to this type of receptacle, strip the wire end, poke it into the terminal hole, and tighten the setscrew. Fasten the receptacle body to the floor or wall and install the cover.

Dryer receptacle

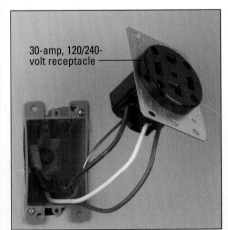

1 Install 10/3 NM cable or run four #10 wires through conduit or Greenfield cable from the service panel to a receptacle box *(pages 42–53)*. Connect the wires to the terminals of the receptacle.

2 At the service panel, **shut off the main breaker.** Connect the ground and white wires to the grounding and neutral bus bars. Connect the black and red wires to a double-pole breaker and snap in the breaker.

STANLEY PRO TIP

Use a whip

To connect to a cooktop or a wall-mounted oven, run cable from the service panel to a junction box. Connect an appliance whip—a short length of armored cable—to the junction box and to the appliance (see *page 111)*. Some new appliances come with a whip already attached to the unit.

Keep it neat—and safe

If wires enter far from the breaker, route them around the perimeter of the panel. This eases future work in the panel, clarifies the circuitry, and avoids strain on connections.

TWO-CIRCUIT RECEPTACLES

Code may require that receptacles supplying several high-amperage appliances or tools be placed on alternating circuits. That way, if an appliance causes a circuit to overload, you can simply plug it into a neighboring receptacle. Another option is to split the receptacles *(page 63)*.

Run three-wire cable from the service panel to the boxes *(pages 42–53)*. If codes call for 20-amp receptacles, use #12 wire. Codes may also call for connecting both circuits to the same double-pole breaker. That way, if one circuit overloads, both circuits will shut off, ensuring that all wires in each box are dead.

PRESTART CHECKLIST

☐ **TIME**
About three hours to install several receptacles (not including cutting and patching walls)

☐ **TOOLS**
Voltage tester, drill, saw, hammer, fish tape, lineman's pliers, screwdriver, strippers, longnose pliers

☐ **SKILLS**
Running cable; stripping, splicing, connecting wire

☐ **PREP**
Run three-wire cable from service panel to boxes; two-wire between last two boxes

☐ **MATERIALS**
Receptacles, three-wire cable, two-wire cable, boxes, double-pole breaker, wire nuts, tape

Blacks to brass terminals

Reds to brass terminals

1 **Shut off power to the circuits.** At the first receptacle, splice the red wires. Connect the grounds. Attach the white wires to the silver terminals. Connect the black wires to the brass terminals.

2 At the second receptacle, splice the black wires. Connect the grounds. Attach the white wires to the silver terminals. Connect the red wires to the brass terminals.

3 At the service panel, **shut off the main breaker.** Connect the white wire and the ground wire to the neutral and ground bus bars. Attach the red and black wires to a double-pole breaker.

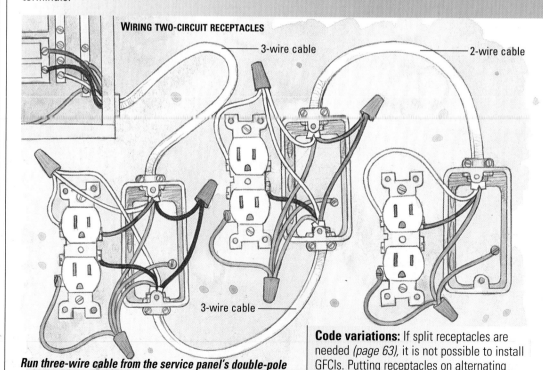

WIRING TWO-CIRCUIT RECEPTACLES

3-wire cable

2-wire cable

3-wire cable

Run three-wire cable from the service panel's double-pole breaker to the receptacles. Only two-wire cable is needed for the last receptacle.

Code variations: If split receptacles are needed *(page 63)*, it is not possible to install GFCIs. Putting receptacles on alternating circuits allows you to use GFCI receptacles.

SPLIT RECEPTACLES

If a receptacle is split, its two plugs are on separate circuits. If an appliance or tool causes a circuit to overload, just plug into the other outlet of the same receptacle. It's also possible to split a receptacle and have one outlet controlled by a switch (see *pages 64–65*).

Run three-wire cable from the service panel to the receptacle boxes *(pages 42–53)*. If codes call for 20-amp receptacles, use #12 wire. Codes may also call for connecting both circuits to the same double-pole breaker. That way, if one circuit overloads, both circuits will be shut off, ensuring that all the wires in each box are dead.

PRESTART CHECKLIST

☐ **TIME**
About three hours to install several receptacles (not including cutting and patching walls)

☐ **TOOLS**
Voltage tester, drill, saw, hammer, fish tape, screwdriver, strippers, longnose pliers, lineman's pliers

☐ **SKILLS**
Running cable; stripping, splicing, connecting wire

☐ **PREP**
Run three-wire cable from service panel to boxes

☐ **MATERIALS**
Receptacles, three-wire cable, boxes, double-pole breaker, wire nuts, electrician's tape

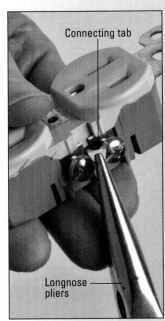

Connecting tab

Longnose pliers

1 On each receptacle, twist off the tab that connects the two brass terminals. Now the two outlets are disconnected from each other.

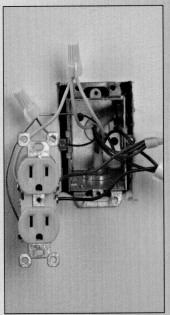

2 Make certain no power is present in the cable or boxes. At each receptacle, pigtail the red, black, and white wires. Connect the red and black pigtails to separate brass terminals and connect the white pigtail to a silver terminal.

Double-pole breaker

3 At the service panel, shut off the main breaker. Connect the white wire and the ground wire to the neutral and ground bus bars. Connect the red and black wires to a double-pole breaker.

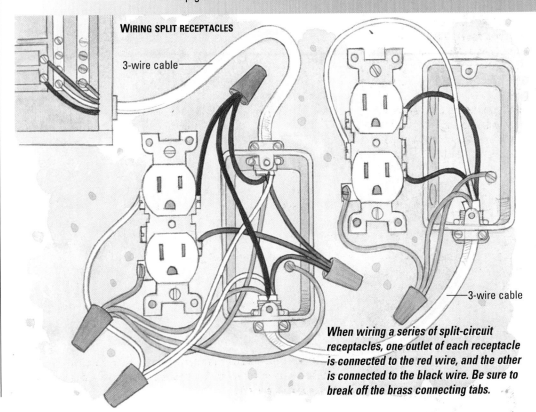

WIRING SPLIT RECEPTACLES

3-wire cable

3-wire cable

When wiring a series of split-circuit receptacles, one outlet of each receptacle is connected to the red wire, and the other is connected to the black wire. Be sure to break off the brass connecting tabs.

SWITCHED RECEPTACLES

A receptacle can be split and switched, so that one of its outlets is controlled by a wall switch while the other remains hot all the time. If a floor or table lamp is plugged into the switched plug, you can turn it on as you enter a room. Many codes allow a bedroom to have no ceiling light, as long as there is a switched receptacle.

The steps on these pages show how to split and switch an existing receptacle that is wired normally. If you need to install a new receptacle and switch, see the illustration on *page 65.*

If the wall is covered with drywall or plaster, most of the work will consist of running cable and perhaps patching the wall afterwards *(pages 48–55).*

PRESTART CHECKLIST

☐ **TIME**
About three hours to run cable a short distance (not including cutting a pathway for the cable and patching walls), install a wall switch, and wire the receptacle

☐ **TOOLS**
Voltage tester, drill, saw, hammer, nonconductive ladder, fish tape, screwdriver, strippers, longnose pliers, lineman's pliers

☐ **SKILLS**
Stripping, splicing, and connecting wires to terminals; installing boxes; running cable through walls

☐ **PREP**
Lay a drop cloth on the floor below

☐ **MATERIALS**
Single-pole switch, receptacle (if you want to replace the old one), two-wire cable, wire nuts, remodel box, cable clamps, electrician's tape

1 **Shut off power to the circuit.** Without touching the terminals, carefully pull out the existing receptacle and test for power.

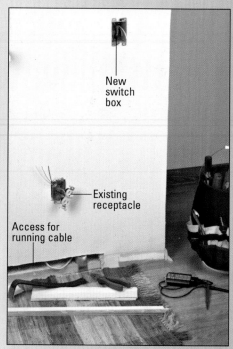

2 Cut a hole for a switch box, run cable from the hole to the existing receptacle box, and clamp the cable to the box *(pages 42–53).*

IF POWER ENTERS THE RECEPTACLE BOX

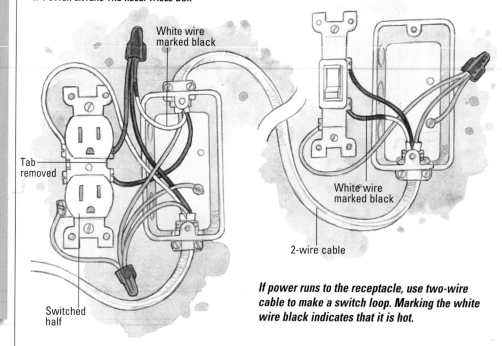

If power runs to the receptacle, use two-wire cable to make a switch loop. Marking the white wire black indicates that it is hot.

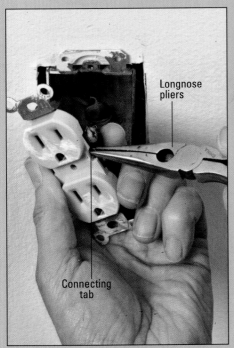

3 Either remove and replace the receptacle or continue to use the existing one. Remove the tab that connects the two brass terminals; now the two outlets are no longer connected to each other.

4 At the receptacle, mark the white switch wire with black tape and connect the grounds. Splice the feed wire with the black-marked wire and a pigtail. Connect the pigtail to a brass terminal, the remaining black wire to the other brass terminal, and the white wire to a silver terminal.

5 If only one cable originally entered the switch box, connect the ground and mark the white switch wire with black tape. Connect the wires to the switch terminals.

If power enters the switch box

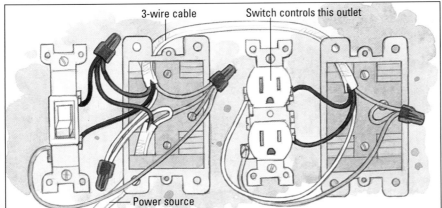

If you are installing a new receptacle and switch, this is the most common configuration. Bring power to the switch box via two-wire cable and run three-wire cable between the boxes. Connect the grounds. At the switch box, splice the white wires. Splice the black wires together with a pigtail and connect the pigtail to a terminal. Connect the red wire to a terminal. At the receptacle, connect the red and black wires to brass terminals and the white wire to a silver terminal.

WHAT IF…
A receptacle is middle of the run?

If two cables originally entered the receptacle box, connect the grounds and mark the white switch wire black. Attach the black switch wire to one brass terminal. Splice the remaining black wires and the white switch wire together with a pigtail. Connect the pigtail to the other brass terminal. Connect the remaining white wires to silver terminals.

INSTALLING A NEW SWITCHED FIXTURE

A switched fixture can be hooked up in one of two ways: Through-switch or in-line wiring (shown in the steps at right) brings power first to the switch, then sends it on to the fixture; the switch interrupts the hot wire that leads to the fixture. End-line or switch-loop wiring (shown at the bottom of *page 67)* brings power first to the fixture; two-wire cable running from the fixture to the switch creates a loop that is interrupted by the switch.

Some inspectors prefer through-switch wiring, but both methods work equally well. Unless your inspector objects, choose the wiring method that makes for the easiest cable runs.

These two pages give instructions for installing a simple fixture with a switch. For various switch-receptacle-fixture combinations, see *pages 68–69.*

PRESTART CHECKLIST

☐ **TIME**
About two hours to run cable and install a switch and a receptacle (not including cutting a pathway for the cable and patching walls)

☐ **TOOLS**
Voltage tester, drill, saw, hammer, nonconductive ladder, fish tape, screwdriver, strippers, longnose pliers, lineman's pliers

☐ **SKILLS**
Stripping, splicing, and connecting wires to terminals; installing boxes; running cable into boxes

☐ **PREP**
Lay a drop cloth on the floor below

☐ **MATERIALS**
Single-pole switch, light fixture or ceiling fan, two-wire cable, ceiling box, cable clamps, wall box, wire nuts, electrician's tape

1 Before tapping into a power source *(pages 42–43),* list all the electrical users on the circuit and add up the wattages to see whether there is room on the circuit for a new light switch. See *pages 24–25.*

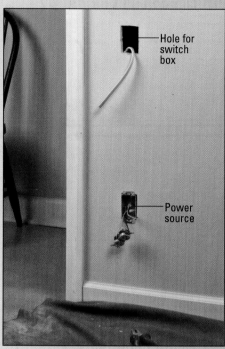

2 Cut a hole for the switch box, and run two-wire cable from the hole to a power source. In this example, a receptacle directly below the switch makes for an easy cable run. *Pages 42–53* show how to install boxes and run cable.

THROUGH-SWITCH WIRING

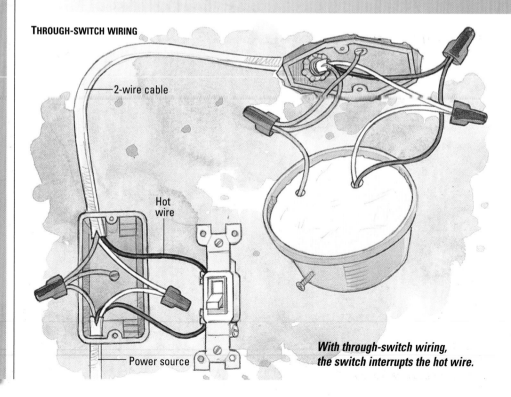

2-wire cable

Hot wire

Power source

With through-switch wiring, the switch interrupts the hot wire.

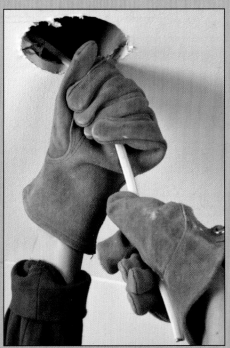

3 Cut a hole for the ceiling fixture box and run two-wire cable from that hole to the switch hole.

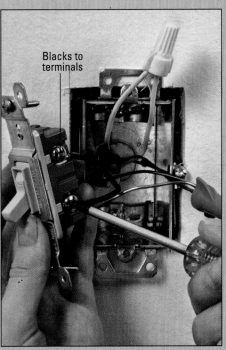

Blacks to terminals

4 At the switch hole, strip and clamp the cables in a box and install the box. Connect the grounds. Splice the white wires and connect the black wires to the switch terminals.

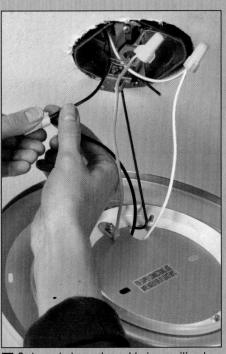

5 Strip and clamp the cable in a ceiling box and install the box. Connect the grounds. Splice the white wire to the white fixture lead and the black wire to the black lead.

END-LINE WIRING

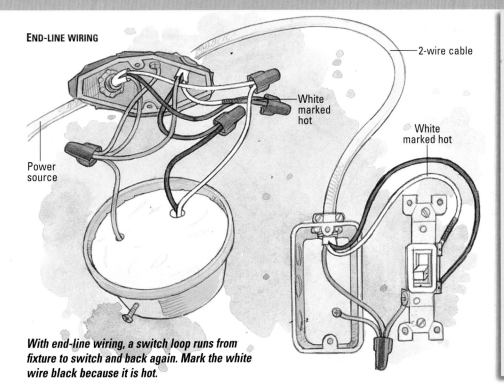

2-wire cable

White marked hot

White marked hot

Power source

With end-line wiring, a switch loop runs from fixture to switch and back again. Mark the white wire black because it is hot.

STANLEY PRO TIP

Switching a pull-chain fixture

To control a pull-chain fixture with a wall switch, run two-wire cable from the fixture to a switch box. Connect wires as for end-line wiring, left.

Switch, light, and receptacle

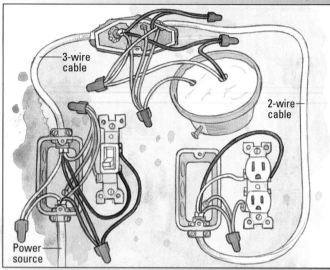

This setup has a switched fixture and an unswitched receptacle. Bring power into the switch box with two-wire cable; run three-wire cable to the fixture and run two-wire cable to the receptacle. Connect all the grounds. At the switch box, connect the black and red wires to the switch terminal and splice the white wires. At the fixture box, splice the black wires and splice the white wires together with the white fixture lead. Splice the red wire to the black fixture lead. Wire the receptacle.

End-line option

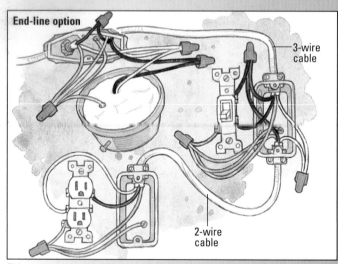

Bring power to the fixture via two-wire cable; run three-wire cable to the switch and run two-wire cable from the switch to the receptacle. Connect all the grounds. At the fixture box, splice the black wires and splice the white wires together with the white fixture lead. Splice the red wire to the black fixture lead. At the switch box, splice the white wires and splice the black wires together with a pigtail. Connect the black pigtail and the red wire to the switch terminals. Wire the receptacle.

Two fixtures on two switches

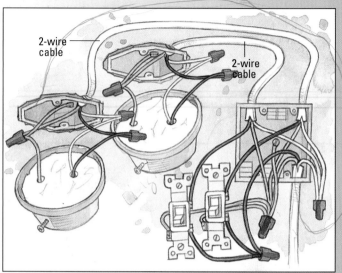

Here, two switches, each of which controls a separate light, share a double-gang box. Bring power into the switch box via two-wire cable and run two-wire cable to each of the fixtures. Connect all the grounds. At the switch box, connect the feed wire to the switches, using pigtails. Connect each black fixture wire to a switch and splice the white wires. Wire the fixtures.

End-line option

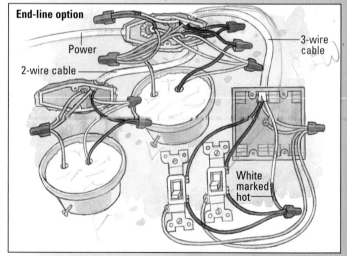

Bring power to the first fixture box with two-wire cable. Run two-wire cable between the fixtures; run three-wire cable from the first fixture to the switch box. Connect the grounds. At the first fixture box, mark the white switch wire black and splice it to the feed wire. Splice the other two black wires. Splice the remaining white wires with the white fixture lead. Splice the red wire with the black fixture lead. Wire the other fixture. At the switch box, connect the red wire to one switch and the black wire to the other. Mark the white wire black and connect it to the switches with pigtails.

Switch and two or more fixtures

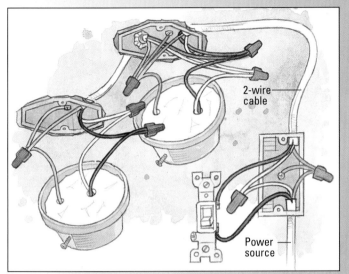

Here, a single switch controls two fixtures. Run two-wire cable into all the boxes. Connect all the grounds. At the switch box, splice the white wires and connect the black wires to the switch terminals. At the first fixture box, splice the two black wires with the fixture's black lead and splice the two white wires with the fixture's white lead. Wire the second fixture.

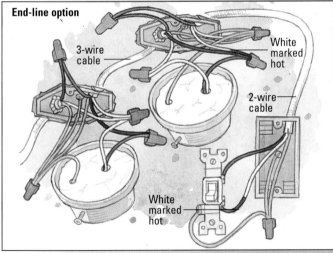

Bring power into the first fixture box with two-wire cable; run three-wire cable between the fixture boxes and run two-wire cable from the second fixture box to the switch box. Connect all the grounds. At the first fixture box, splice the black wires. Splice the white wires together with the white fixture lead and splice the red wire with the black fixture lead. At the second fixture box, splice the black wires. Mark the white fixture wire with black tape and splice it together with the red wire and the black fixture lead. Splice the white wire to the white fixture lead. Wire the switch.

Switch and receptacle

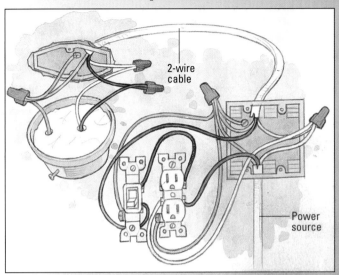

Here, a switch and an always-hot receptacle share a double-gang box. Run two-wire cable to both boxes. Connect all the grounds. At the switch box, connect the feed wire to a brass receptacle terminal. Run a short black wire from the other brass terminal to a switch terminal. Splice the white wires together with a pigtail and connect the pigtail to a silver receptacle terminal. Connect the black fixture wire to the remaining switch terminal. Wire the fixture.

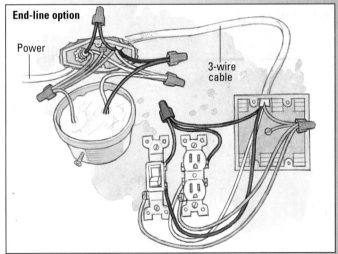

Bring power to the fixture box with two-wire cable; run three-wire cable from the fixture box to the switch box. Connect all the grounds. At the fixture box, splice the black wires. Splice the white wires together with the white fixture lead and splice the red wire with the black lead. At the switch box, connect the black wire to a switch terminal and a brass receptacle terminal, using pigtails. Connect the red wire to a switch terminal and connect the white wire to a silver receptacle terminal.

INSTALLING THREE-WAY SWITCHES

Install a pair of three-way switches to control a fixture from two different locations. A three-way switch has three terminals: two traveler terminals and one common terminal, which is darker in color. The toggle is not marked ON and OFF, because flipping it down could turn a light on. Use three-ways to ensure that a person does not have to walk through the dark to get to the light switch. Install three-ways in hallways and stairways, in large rooms with two entrances, or to control a garage or basement light. These pages give instructions for one possible way to wire three-ways—with power entering a switch and traveling through the fixture to the other switch. *Pages 72–73* present three more possibilities and discuss four-way switches as well. Choose the setup that makes it easiest for you to run the cable.

PRESTART CHECKLIST

☐ **TIME**
About four hours to run cable and install a light and two switches (not including cutting a pathway and patching walls)

☐ **TOOLS**
Voltage tester, drill, saw, hammer, screwdriver, ladder, fish tape, strippers, longnose pliers, lineman's pliers

☐ **SKILLS**
Stripping, splicing, connecting wires to terminals; installing boxes; running cable through walls and ceilings

☐ **PREP**
Check that a new fixture won't overload the circuit and tap into a power source. Lay a drop cloth on the floor below.

☐ **MATERIALS**
Two-wire and three-wire cable, ceiling fixture, two three-way switches, switch and fixture boxes, cable clamps, wire nuts, tape

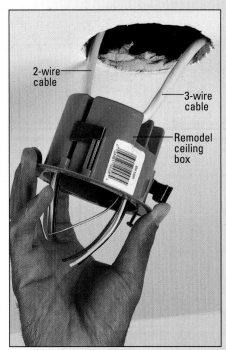

1 Shut off power to the circuit. Cut holes for two wall boxes and a ceiling box. Run two-wire cable from the power source to the first switch box, three-wire cable to the ceiling box, and three-wire cable to the second switch box *(pages 42–53.)*

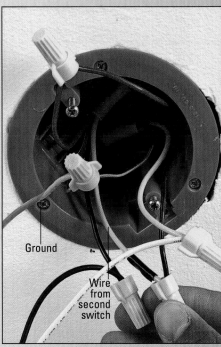

2 Clamp cable to all three boxes. Install all the boxes and connect all the grounds. At the fixture box, splice the red wires. Mark the white wire from the second switch with black tape.

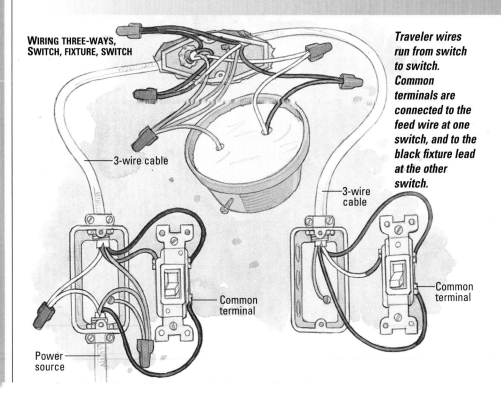

WIRING THREE-WAYS,
SWITCH, FIXTURE, SWITCH

Traveler wires run from switch to switch. Common terminals are connected to the feed wire at one switch, and to the black fixture lead at the other switch.

3-wire cable

3-wire cable

Common terminal

Common terminal

Power source

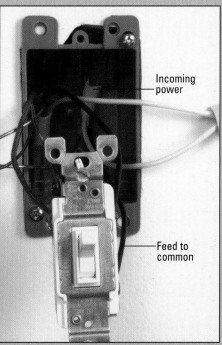

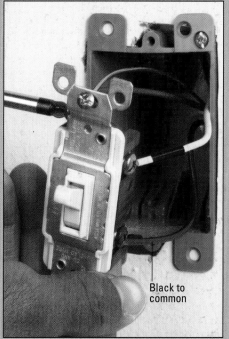

3 Splice the black-marked white wire with the black wire from the first switch. Splice the remaining black and white wires with the fixture's black and white leads.

4 At the first switch (where power enters), splice the white wires. Connect the feed wire to the common terminal and the remaining red and black wires to the traveler terminals.

5 At the second switch, mark the white wire with black tape. Connect the black wire to the common terminal. Connect the red wire and the black-marked white wire to the traveler terminals.

How three-ways work

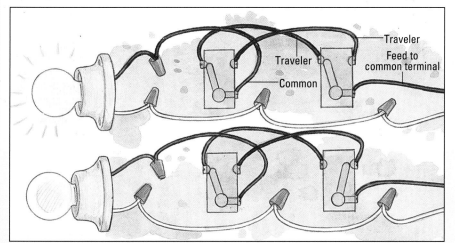

In a three-way setup, the light is turned on when power can flow through both switches to the fixture. If the circuit is broken at either switch, the light is turned off. Traveler wires run from switch to switch and do not connect to the fixture. Common wires bring power to the fixture.

STANLEY PRO TIP

Three rules for three-ways

If a wiring diagram gets confusing, pause a minute and ponder these rules:
■ Route traveler wires so they run from traveler terminals to traveler terminals and never to the fixture.
■ Attach the feed wire to the common terminal of one switch.
■ At the other switch, the wire connecting to the common terminal should lead to the black fixture lead.

Where three-ways are required
Codes require all lights in hallways and stairways to be controlled with three-way switches.

Switch, switch, fixture

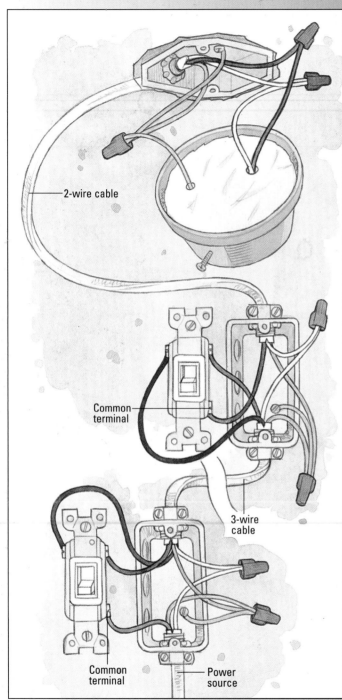

2-wire cable

Common terminal

3-wire cable

Common terminal

Power source

At the first switch, connect the feed wire to the common terminal, splice the white wires, and connect red and black wires to traveler terminals. At the second switch, connect the travelers to the traveler terminals and the black wire from the fixture to the common terminal. At the fixture, splice the white lead with the white wire, the black lead with the black wire from the switch's common terminal.

Fixture, radiating to switches

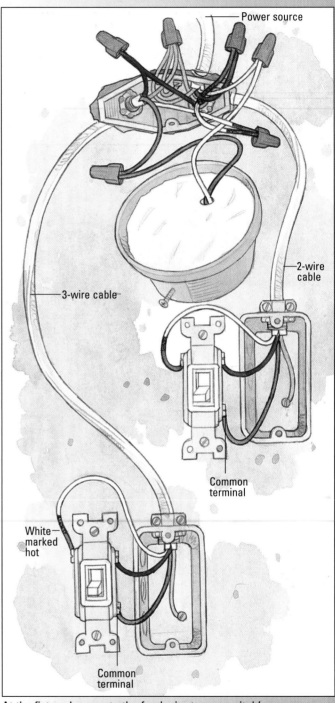

Power source

3-wire cable

2-wire cable

Common terminal

White-marked hot

Common terminal

At the fixture box, route the feed wire to one switch's common terminal. Red and black-marked white wires travel from switch to switch. Splice the fixture's white lead with the white wire and the black lead with the black wire coming from the other switch's common terminal.

Fixture, switch, switch

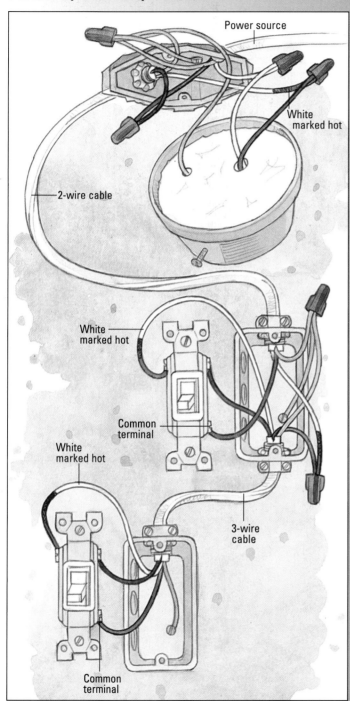

Route the feed wire to the first switch's common terminal. The black wire on the second switch's common terminal runs via a black-marked white wire to the fixture's black lead. A red wire and a black-marked white wire travel from switch to switch.

Four-way wiring

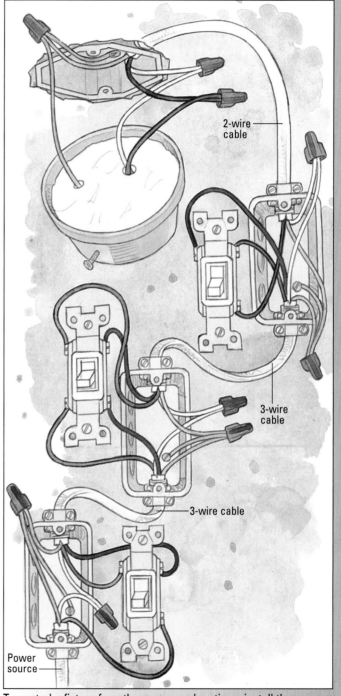

To control a fixture from three or more locations, install three-way switches at each end and one or more four-ways in between. A four-way switch has only traveler terminals and no common terminal. Connect wires from the first switch to the "input" terminals; wires connected to the "output" terminals lead to the third switch.

UNDERCABINET FLUORESCENTS

Home centers carry a variety of lights designed to fit under cabinets to illuminate a countertop without shining in the food preparer's eyes. Plug-in lights (either fluorescent or low-voltage halogens) with their own switches are the simplest to install, but are not as convenient to use as a string of fluorescent lights controlled by a single wall switch.

When remodeling a kitchen, the wall cabinets are removed (shown). If wall cabinets are in place, see *page 75* for tips on snaking cable so as to minimize damage to walls.

Some undercabinet fluorescent lights have a single outlet, which comes in handy if the wall beneath is short on receptacles. Thin fixtures (1-inch thick) are more difficult to wire than standard (1½-inch thick) fixtures.

PRESTART CHECKLIST

☐ **TIME**
About half a day to cut holes and run cable and another half-day to install the lights after the cabinets are up

☐ **TOOLS**
Voltage tester, drill, hammer, drywall saw, level, stud finder, fish tape, screwdriver, strippers, longnose pliers, lineman's pliers

☐ **SKILLS**
Stripping, splicing, and connecting wires to terminals; installing boxes; running cable through walls and ceilings

☐ **PREP**
Find power source and check that the new lights will not overload the circuit *(pages 24–25)*. Clear the room of all debris and lay a drop cloth on the floor.

☐ **MATERIALS**
Fluorescent under-cabinet fixtures, cable, remodel box with clamps, single-pole switch, wire nuts, tape

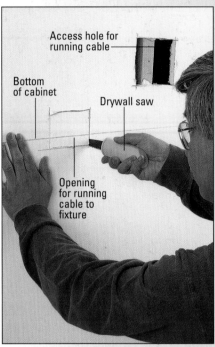

1 On the wall, use a level to draw the exact locations of the cabinets. Determine how the lights will fit onto the cabinets; you may need to cut a lip at the bottom of the cabinets. Cut access holes in the walls. Make sure all holes will be covered by the cabinets.

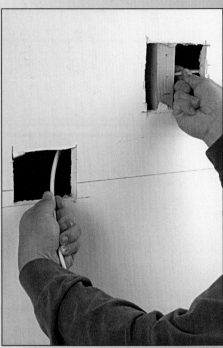

2 Shut off power to the circuit. Run cable from the switch hole to a power source *(pages 42–43)*. Run cables from the switch box to the fixture holes *(pages 48–53)*. Leave at least 16 inches of cable hanging out from each fixture hole.

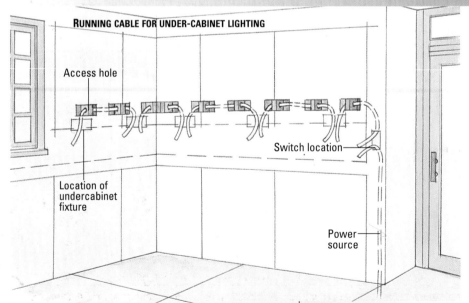

RUNNING CABLE FOR UNDER-CABINET LIGHTING

Access hole

Location of undercabinet fixture

Switch location

Power source

In this installation, the lights will mount against the wall and will cover the holes. Cable runs from the power source to the switch, then to each fixture. To make sure the gap between lights is never more than 6 inches, you may need to purchase lights of various lengths.

Check local code
Code may call for armored cable or require a box for each fixture.

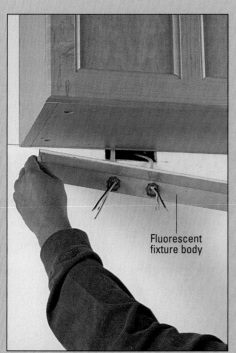

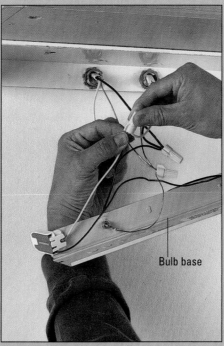

Fluorescent fixture body

Bulb base

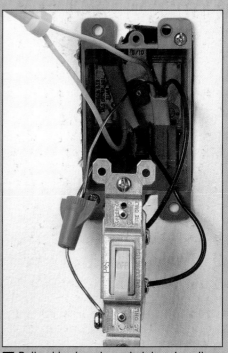

3 If the cabinet has a lip at the bottom, cut or drill a hole in it for the cable to pass through. After the cabinets are installed, strip sheathing and clamp the cables to the fixture body *(pages 34–37)*.

4 At each fixture, connect the grounds. Splice black wires with the black fixture lead and white wires with the white fixture lead. Once connected, position and fold the wires carefully so they do not make contact with the ballast.

5 Pull cables into the switch box, install the box, and wire the switch. Connect the grounds and splice the white wires together. Connect the black wires to the switch terminals.

Two ways to run cable with cabinets in place

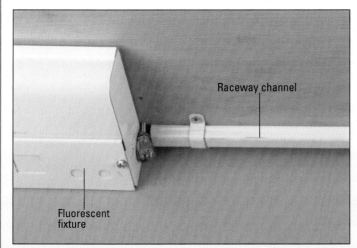

Raceway channel

Fluorescent fixture

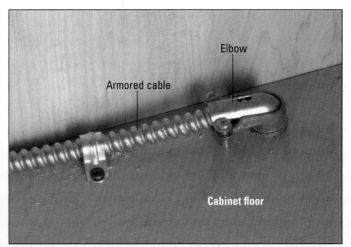

Elbow

Armored cable

Cabinet floor

If removing the cabinets is not practical, consult with your inspector for the best way to run wiring. One option is to run wires through metal or plastic raceway channels attached to the underside of the cabinets.

Or run armored cable through the inside of the cabinet. Use elbows to bring the wiring down to the light fixtures from the top, rather than the side. Both methods call for precise cutting of channels or cable sheathing.

RECESSED CANS

The most inconspicuous way to illuminate a large room is to install a series of recessed canister lights, also called "cans" or "pot lights." Install a grid of lights spaced 6 to 8 feet apart. Use eyeball-type can lights to highlight wall features, task lights to brighten a countertop or sink, and a watertight recessed fixture above a tub or shower.

Remodel can lights are easy to install in finished walls. Even running cable is not too difficult, because cans are usually spaced only two or three joists apart. Using a fishing drill bit *(page 53)*, you may need to cut only a few holes in the ceiling.

See *page 78* for tips on buying recessed lights. Most inexpensive recessed cans are rated to use only 60-watt bulbs.

PRESTART CHECKLIST

☐ **TIME**
About a day to cut holes, run cable, and install six to eight lights with a switch

☐ **TOOLS**
Voltage tester, drill, spade bit or fishing drill bit, stud finder, ladder, saw, level, hammer, fish tape, screwdriver, strippers, longnose pliers, lineman's pliers

☐ **SKILLS**
Precision cutting of drywall or plaster; stripping, splicing, and connecting wires to terminals; installing boxes; running cable through walls and ceilings

☐ **PREP**
Find power source and make sure that the new lights will not overload the circuit *(pages 24–25, 42–43)*. Clear the room of all obstructions and lay a drop cloth on the floor.

☐ **MATERIALS**
Recessed canister lights, cable, switch box and clamps, wire nuts, electrician's tape

A. Rough-in the wiring

Mark center of fixture.

Template

1 Plan the locations for the lights and draw lines marking the center of each. Use a stud finder or a bent wire *(page 77)* to see if a joist is in the way. You can move the light several inches to avoid a joist—the inconsistency won't be noticeable.

2 Center the hole in the cardboard template over your location mark. Holding the template in place, mark your cut line.

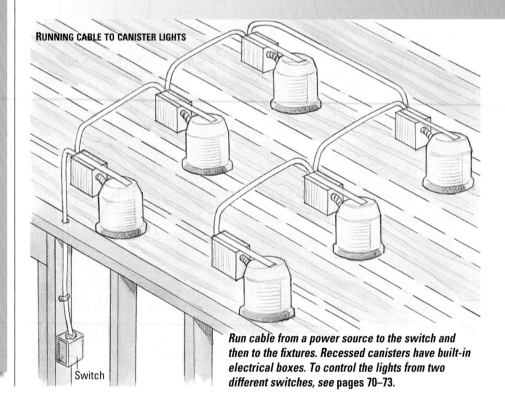

RUNNING CABLE TO CANISTER LIGHTS

Switch

Run cable from a power source to the switch and then to the fixtures. Recessed canisters have built-in electrical boxes. To control the lights from two different switches, see pages 70–73.

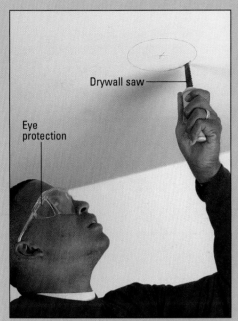

Eye protection

Drywall saw

¾-inch spade bit

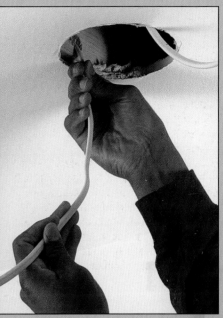

3 Cut the hole with a drywall saw. Wear safety glasses because drywall dust stings terribly if it gets in eyes. If the ceiling is plaster, see *page 48* for cutting tips. Cut precisely—the canister trim leaves little room for error.

4 Drill holes for the cable as far up the joist as possible so drywall nails cannot reach the cable. See *pages 48–53* for tips on running cable through walls and ceilings.

5 Run cable up from the power source to the switch box, then run cable to each fixture hole (see the illustration on *page 76*). Allow at least 16 inches of cable to hang down from each hole.

STANLEY PRO TIP

Bent wire test

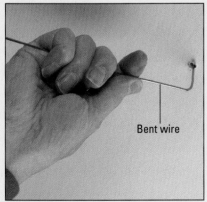

Bent wire

To make sure the fixture will not bump into a joist, use a stud finder. Or drill a ¼-inch hole, insert a bent wire, and spin the wire around to see whether you encounter an obstruction.

WHAT IF...
The ceiling framing is exposed?

If the ceiling joists are not covered with drywall or plaster, install a new-work can light. Adjust the light to accommodate the thickness of the drywall that will be put up later. Slide the mounting bars out and hammer each tab into a joist. Slide the light to position it precisely.

Mapping can lights

With a standard flood bulb, a recessed light will illuminate an area about as wide as the ceiling is high. Make a scale drawing of your room and map a grid of lights that are at least fairly consistent in their spacing.

■ If your ceiling is 8 feet high, a typical recessed light will shine on a floor area with a diameter of 8 feet (a radius of 4 feet). To light the room, install a grid of lights spaced no more than 8 feet apart. The perimeter lights should be no more than 4 feet from the walls. Lights placed closer together—perhaps 6 or 7 feet apart and only 2–3 feet from the walls—will more fully light the room.

■ If you have a 10-foot ceiling, lights can be 7 to 10 feet apart and as much as 5 feet from the wall.

B. Install the lights

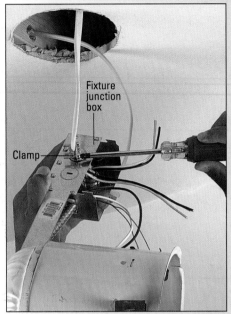

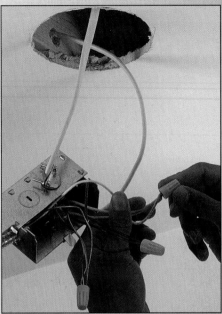

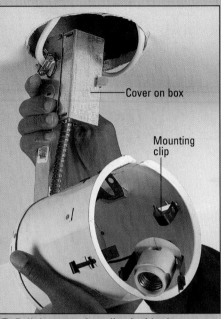

Fixture junction box

Clamp

Cover on box

Mounting clip

1 Strip about 6 inches of sheathing from the cable. Remove the cover from the fixture junction box and twist off a knockout for each cable. Slide the cable in and clamp the cable.

2 Connect the grounds. Splice white wires with white leads and black wires with black leads. Fold the wires into the junction box and replace the cover.

3 Pull the mounting clips inside the can so they will not be in the way when you push the canister into the hole. Without tangling the cables, guide the junction box through the hole and push in the canister.

STANLEY PRO TIP

"IC" light near insulation

If insulation will come within 3 inches of a recessed light, be sure to install a fixture rated "IC" (insulation compatible). A non-IC light will overheat dangerously.

WHAT IF...
Ceiling space is sloped or tight?

If the ceiling is sloped, buy special canisters that are adjustable so the light can point straight down.

If the vertical space above the ceiling is less than 8 inches, buy a low-clearance fixture. Some are small enough to fit into a space only 4 inches high.

Compact low-voltage halogen can lights are expensive, but they present new style options and produce an intense light.

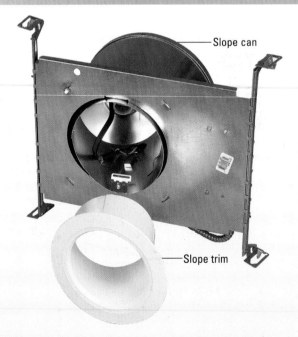

Slope can

Slope trim

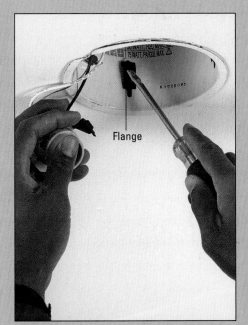

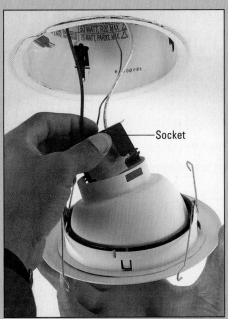

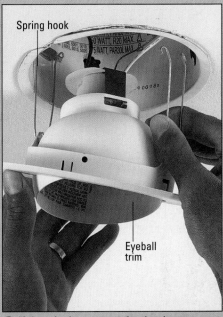

4 Push the canister so its flange is tight to the ceiling. With a slot screwdriver, push up each mounting clip until it clicks into place, clamping the canister to the drywall or plaster.

5 Many canisters have sockets that attach to the trim with two spring clips. Slip one clip into the notch provided and rock the socket so the clip engages.

6 If the trim has two spring hooks, squeeze and guide their ends into the slots provided, then push up the trim until it snaps into place. Twist an eyeball trim to face in the desired direction.

WHAT IF...
The canister has a spring-hook?

To mount trim that uses coil springs (shown), hold the trim in place up against the ceiling. Insert a pencil tip into the looped end of each spring and guide it up into the hole provided.

Trim options

Baffle trim (either white or black) diffuses the light, while reflector trim increases the brightness of a bulb. With open trim, the flood bulb protrudes slightly downward. For above a tub or shower, choose a watertight lens. An eyeball (or fish-eye) trim rotates to point where you want it; a wallwasher highlights the texture of a brick or stone wall.

Baffle trim

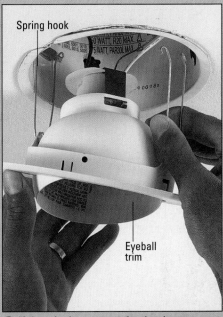

Reflector trim

Open trim

Flush watertight lens

Wallwasher trim

Eyeball trim

Extended watertight lens

WALL-MOUNTED LIGHTING

Wall sconces provide indirect lighting ideal for hallways or stairways or on a large wall where a modest accent is needed. Place them just above eye level.

Use a standard ceiling box and wire just as you would a ceiling light. Most sconces mount with a center stud so you can adjust the fixture for level even if the box is not level. To control sconces from two locations, use three-way switches *(pages 70–73)*.

The two fixtures on both sides of a mirror *(page 57)* install just like sconces.

A strip of lights over a bathroom mirror or medicine chest calls for a similar installation method. Such fixtures use several low-wattage bulbs to reduce glare while providing plenty of light.

PRESTART CHECKLIST

☐ **TIME**
About three hours to run cable and install a switch and two sconces (not including cutting a pathway for the cable and patching walls)

☐ **TOOLS**
Voltage tester, drill, saw, hammer, fish tape, screwdriver, strippers, longnose pliers, lineman's pliers

☐ **SKILLS**
Stripping, splicing, and connecting wires to terminals; installing boxes; running cable through walls and ceilings

☐ **PREP**
Find power source and make sure that the new lights will not overload the circuit *(pages 24–25, 42–43)*. Spread a drop cloth on the floor below.

☐ **MATERIALS**
Sconce(s), ceiling boxes and a switch box with clamps, cable, switch, wire nuts, electrician's tape

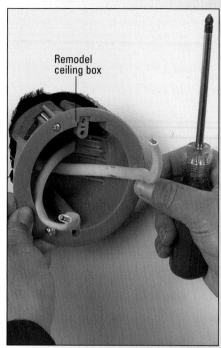

1 **Shut off power to the circuit.** Cut holes for the sconce boxes and the switch. Run cable from the power source to the switch then to the sconces *(pages 48–53)*.

2 Clamp cable to a wall box and install the box. Most sconces come with all the necessary hardware—usually a strap with a center stud. If the strap is provided, use it; it helps carry heat away from the fixture.

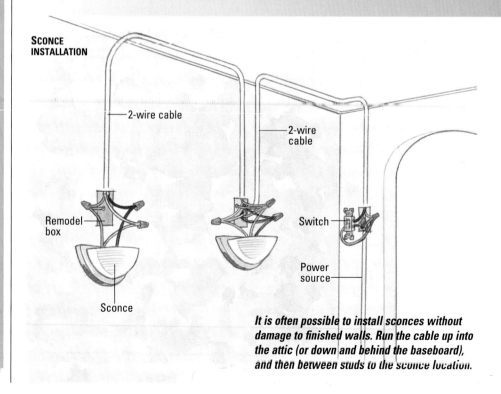

SCONCE INSTALLATION

2-wire cable

2-wire cable

Remodel box

Switch

Power source

Sconce

It is often possible to install sconces without damage to finished walls. Run the cable up into the attic (or down and behind the baseboard), and then between studs to the sconce location.

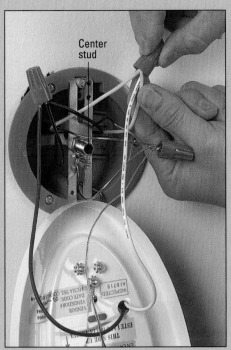

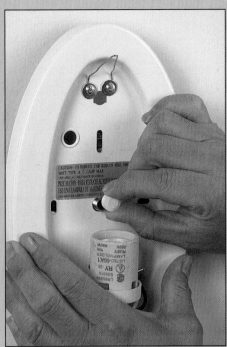

3 To wire a sconce, connect the grounds. Splice the white fixture lead to the white wire(s), and the black lead to the black wire(s).

4 Slip the sconce over the center stud, and start to tighten the nut. Stand back and check that the base is plumb, and then tighten the base.

5 Install the light bulb, making sure it does not exceed the manufacturer's recommended wattage. Clip the lens into place. Wire the switch *(pages 67–73)*.

Lights mounted on a mirror

To install a bathroom strip light, center the box over the mirror or medicine chest. Attach the fixture over the box, wire the fixture, and attach the cover.

To install a light fixture directly on a mirror, have a glass supplier cut three holes to match the fixture: a large hole for the electrical box and two smaller holes for mounting screws. Wire the fixture. Apply a thin bead of clear silicone caulk to its back to act as an adhesive. Attach with mounting screws, but don't overtighten them— you might break the mirror.

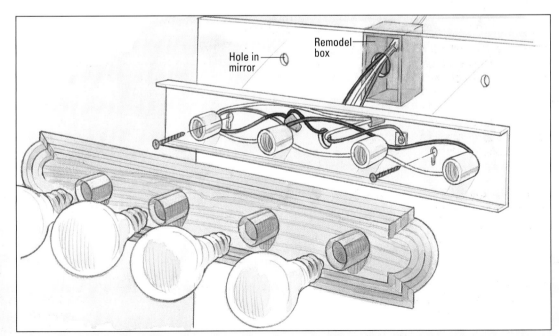

ADDING VENT FANS

Fans that pull air through a room, an attic, or even the whole house contribute to making your home more comfortable, and they reduce energy costs. Small vent fans in the bathroom or kitchen expel unwanted fumes and moisture. Each requires relatively simple wiring; the installation of the fan and ducts or vents require the most time.

An attic must breathe

When the weather is hot and sunny, a stuffy attic can heat up like an oven, making it difficult to cool a house. In cold weather, an attic that is too warm collects moisture that can damage insulation. It can also cause snow on the roof to melt, leading to ice dams at the eaves, which can damage roofing, sheathing, and interior walls and ceilings. The solution to both problems is a well-ventilated attic.

Outside air must circulate freely through an attic. Modern building codes specify types and sizes of attic vents, but an older home may be inadequately vented. An attic should have vents below, at the eaves or the soffit, and above, on the roof, at the ridge, or in the gable. A gable fan or roof fan will pull hot air out of an attic, but only if the eaves or soffit vents are sufficient to allow the air easily to escape.

Choosing the right fan

Ask local builders or home center employees to find out which fan or combination of fans will work best in your house. If your attic is not adequately vented, a gable fan (*pages 88–89*) is usually the easiest way to get the air moving. Install a roof fan (*page 90*) if a gable fan is not feasible. To keep a house cool without turning on the air-conditioning, a whole-house fan (*pages 84–87*) can work wonders. Consult with a dealer to find out which size fan or fans will work most effectively.

If a bathroom stays steamy or a kitchen stays smoky even with a vent fan is on, poorly designed or blocked ductwork may be the culprit (*pages 91 and 94*). Or you may need a more powerful fan.

Built-in fans can reduce cooling costs, remove moisture, and vent unpleasant smoke and odors.

CHAPTER PREVIEW

Whole-house vent fan
page 84

Gable fan
page 88

Roof fan
page 90

Range hood
page 91

Bath vent fan
page 94

If your home does not have adequate eaves, roof, or gable venting, install vents before adding an attic fan. An eaves vent is the easiest to install. Cut a rectangular hole in the soffit, then fasten the vent screen in place with corrosion-resistant screws.

Eaves vent screen

In a well-ventilated attic, air moves up through eaves vents and out through vents on the roof, at the ridge, or in the gable. As an alternative, two large gable vents may do the trick. Always check that vents are cleared of insulation and that items stored in the attic are not blocking air flow.

WHOLE-HOUSE VENTILATING FAN

On mild summer days the gentle air circulation provided by a whole-house fan may be all you need for cooling. The fan pulls fresh air through every room that has an open door or window and sends it out through the attic.

For the fan to work properly, the attic must be adequately vented, and doors or windows must be open in the rooms below. Locate the fan in the ceiling of a top-floor hallway. The one shown on these pages rests on top of an exposed joist. Other models require that you cut a joist and frame an opening—a more complicated project.

In winter, make sure the fan's shutters close tightly and place insulation over the fan so the house won't lose heat.

PRESTART CHECKLIST

☐ **TIME**
About eight hours to run cable and install a fan with a wall switch (not including preparing a path for the cable)

☐ **TOOLS**
Voltage tester, stud finder, drywall saw, drill, circular saw, hammer, fish tape, nonconductive ladder, screwdriver, longnose pliers, lineman's pliers, strippers

☐ **SKILLS**
Splicing and connecting wires to terminals, installing boxes, running cable through walls and ceilings, cutting and attaching boards

☐ **PREP**
Find a power source and make sure that the fan will not overload the circuit (pages 24–25, 42–43). Spread a drop cloth on the floor below. Enlist a helper for lifting and placing the fan.

☐ **MATERIALS**
Whole-house fan, remodel box, switch, electrical boxes with clamps, three-wire cable, wire nuts, electrician's tape

A. Install the fan

3-wire cable for switch

Top plate of wall

1 Cut a hole for the switch box in a wall below the fan. Run three-wire cable down through the ceiling plate to the hole.

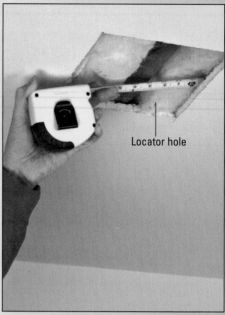

Locator hole

2 Plan to position the fan so it rests on joists at either side; one joist will run through the middle. Use a stud finder to find a center joist, then cut a locator hole and use a tape measure to find the exact location of the joists.

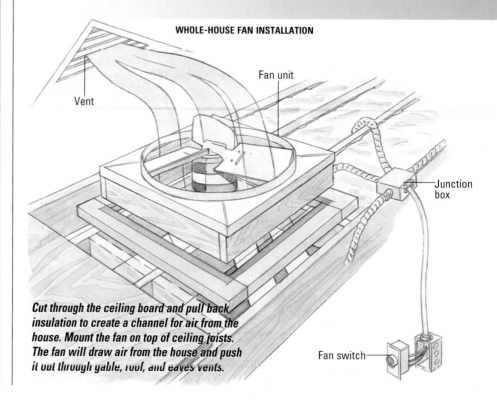

WHOLE-HOUSE FAN INSTALLATION

Vent

Fan unit

Junction box

Fan switch

Cut through the ceiling board and pull back insulation to create a channel for air from the house. Mount the fan on top of ceiling joists. The fan will draw air from the house and push it out through gable, roof, and eaves vents.

Blocking provided with fan

2×4 frame

3 Cut the hole according to manufacturer's directions. Lay pieces of plywood on the attic joists to provide a safe work surface. Work with a helper in the attic to lift the fan up into place.

4 Remove any insulation that's in the way. If blocking is not provided with the fan, cut blocking pieces from lumber the same dimension as your joists. Use the pieces to fill gaps between the joists. Build a frame of 2×4s, lay it flat and square on the joists, and fasten it firmly.

5 Center the fan over the frame. Attach it by driving wood screws (not drywall screws) through the brackets provided and into the frame.

STANLEY PRO TIP

Locating the fan

The best location for a whole-house fan usually is in a top-floor hallway. If the fan is in a room, that room's door must be kept open while the fan is operating. To allow the fan to vent freely, there should be at least 30 inches of vertical space between the joists the fan rests on and the roof rafters. If the attic contains loose insulation, cover it with plastic sheeting.

Open up
Open windows to promote air flow, otherwise the fan will pull air down through the fireplace, water heater, or furnace chimney, which could include carbon monoxide. The back pressure could even shut off a furnace.

Select size and capacity

To cool properly, a whole-house fan should exchange the air in a house at least once every four minutes. The faster the air is exchanged, the cooler the house. Manufacturers offer several sizes of whole-house fans. Find out the total square footage of your home and consult with a salesperson or read the manufacturer's literature to choose the right size for your house. When in doubt, buy the next size up; with a fan-rated multispeed switch, you can always adjust the power downward.

REFRESHER COURSE
Circuit analysis

Take care that your fan will not overload a circuit. Add up the wattages of all the electrical users on the circuit and then add in the fan's wattage. If the total is over 1,440 watts for a 15-amp circuit or 1,920 watts for a 20-amp circuit, the load exceeds "safe capacity." Look for another circuit to tap into (pages 24–25). If you cannot find a circuit with enough available wattage, you may need to run cable all the way back to the service panel and install a new circuit (pages 112–113).

B. Wire the fan

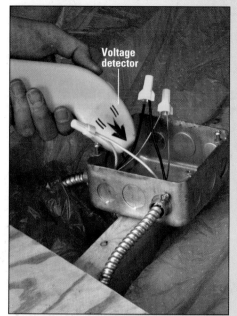

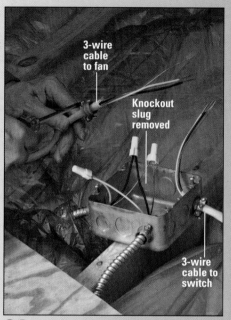

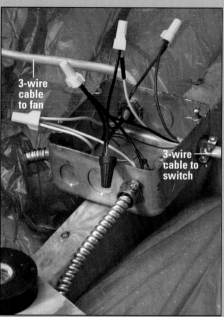

1 **Shut off power to the circuit** you will be using. If there is a junction box in the attic and its circuit can accommodate the fan, pull power from it. If several cables enter the box, **use a voltage detector to make sure all power is off.**

2 Remove knockout slugs and run two three-wire cables, one from the fan and one from the switch *(page 84)*. If the fan comes with a cable "whip" that does not reach the junction box, run it into an intermediate box and run cable from there to the junction box.

3 In the junction box, connect the grounds and splice all white wires in the box, except the one running to the switch. Mark it with black tape and splice it to the black wire running to the fan. Splice together the other black wires and splice the red wires.

SAFETY FIRST
Working safely in an attic

■ If an attic floor is unfinished with exposed insulation and joists, one misstep will put your foot through the ceiling below. Don't take chances; lay down sheets of plywood wherever you will be working.
■ Most insulation—whether fiberglass blankets or loose—is nasty stuff that causes eyes to smart and skin to itch. Wear protective goggles, a dust mask, and long sleeves when cutting or removing it.

Old attic wiring
If you find exposed wires running through porcelain knobs and tubes, the wiring is not necessarily unsafe. However, do not try to grab power from knob-and-tube wiring and take care not to disturb the wires.

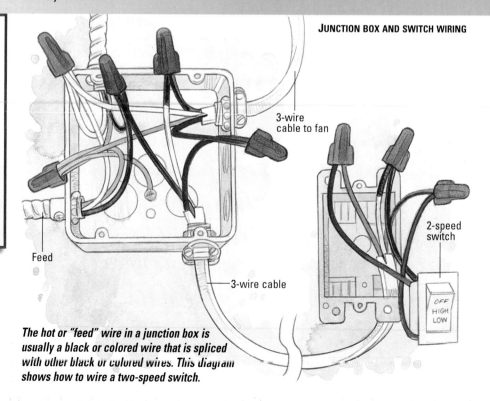

JUNCTION BOX AND SWITCH WIRING

The hot or "feed" wire in a junction box is usually a black or colored wire that is spliced with other black or colored wires. This diagram shows how to wire a two-speed switch.

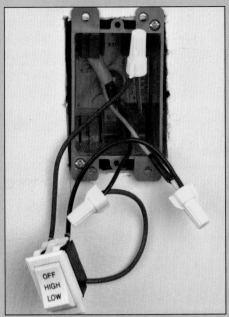

4 At the switch hole, clamp cable to a remodel box and install the box. For the two-speed switch shown above (provided by the fan manufacturer), mark the white wire black with tape and connect it to the black switch lead. Splice the red wire to the red lead and the blue lead to the black wire.

5 Check the fan belt tension. When pressed, it should deflect about ½ inch. If necessary, follow manufacturer's instructions for adjusting the tension. (Not all whole-house fans are belt-driven; some have blades powered directly by the motor.)

6 With a helper, position the shutter so it covers the ceiling hole. Drive screws into joists to attach it firmly to the ceiling. Restore power and test. Be sure the shutter freely opens and closes.

WHAT IF...
There is no power available in the attic?

If there is no usable power source in the attic, run power up through a wall switch and then on to the fan. Check that adding the fan to a nearby fixture or receptacle circuit will not create an overload *(pages 24–25)*. **Shut off power to the circuit** and tap into the power source. Then run cable and install a switch box *(pages 42–43)*. If using a fan-rated rheostat switch, wire it as shown.

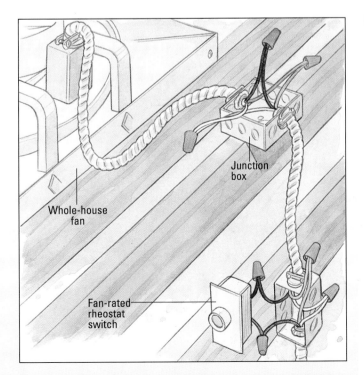

Switch options

In addition to the two-speed switch shown above, switch options include a sliding control with a toggle (which "remembers" the power level when turned on and off), a three-level toggle switch, a three-level sliding switch, a timer, and a pilot light toggle. Make sure any switch is fan-rated.

GABLE FAN

If an attic has a gable (a vertical end wall often pointed at the top), it is usually not difficult to install a fan there. A gable fan is easier to install than roof-mounted fans or vents, which are prone to leak if not sealed correctly.

If your gable does not already have a vent, install one. Plastic louvers are less attractive than fixed wooden units, but they seal out wind and rain more effectively.

Figure the square footage of your attic and total the square footage of your eaves vents. With these two figures in hand, you'll be equipped to shop for a gable fan of the correct size.

Gable fans come with thermostats to turn on automatically when the attic gets too hot and turn off when it cools off.

PRESTART CHECKLIST

☐ **TIME**
About four hours to run cable inside an attic and install a gable fan (not counting additional framing or cutting for gable vent)

☐ **TOOLS**
Voltage tester, drill, drywall saw, circular saw, hammer, screwdriver, strippers, longnose pliers, lineman's pliers

☐ **SKILLS**
Stripping, splicing, connecting wires to terminals, installing rough wood framing

☐ **PREP**
Find power source and make sure the fan will not overload the circuit *(pages 24–25, 42–43)*. Lay sheets of plywood on the attic floor if the joists are exposed. Wear long clothes, protective goggles, and a dust mask.

☐ **MATERIALS**
Gable fan, cable, wood screws, wire nuts, cable clamps, electrician's tape

1 If no gable vent exists, cut and install one *(page 89)*. If the studs are too far apart, add some framing. Cut 2×4s to fit between the studs and attach them with 3-inch screws.

2 Mount the fan on the framing by driving screws through the mounting flanges and into framing members.

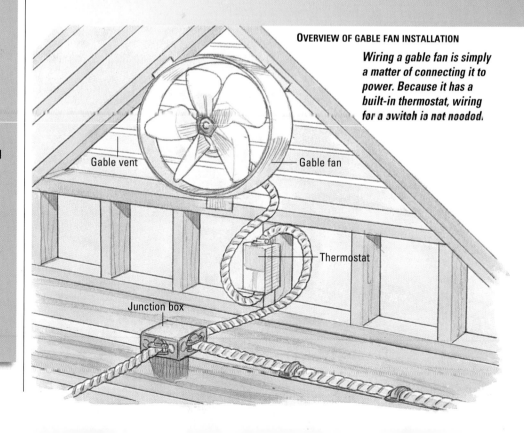

OVERVIEW OF GABLE FAN INSTALLATION

Wiring a gable fan is simply a matter of connecting it to power. Because it has a built-in thermostat, wiring for a switch is not needed.

Gable vent — Gable fan

Thermostat

Junction box

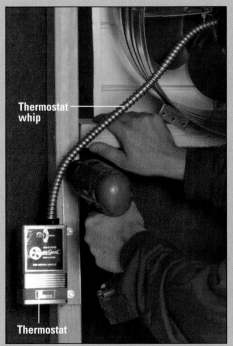

Thermostat whip

Thermostat

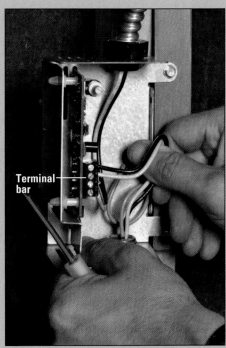

Terminal bar

3 Fasten the fan's thermostat to a framing member. The fan's whip should be taut, so it won't wobble and bang against the framing when the fan is running.

4 Shut off power to the circuit. (To test a junction box for power, see *page 86.*) Run cable from the thermostat into a power source. If no junction box is available in the attic, bring power up from a circuit in the floor below *(pages 42–43, 58)*. Make sure the circuit can handle the additional load.

5 Wire the thermostat following manufacturer's directions. With the thermostat shown above, stripped wire ends are inserted in a terminal bar and screwed tight. Adjust the thermostat control and restore power.

WHAT IF...
No gable vent exists?

Saber saw

Vent shutter

To install a vent shutter, you need not cut or modify framing. Use a saber saw or set a circular saw just deep enough to cut through the siding and sheathing. Cut a hole that will be covered up by the vent frame. Attach the louver by driving screws through its frame and into framing members.

Working with vinyl siding

Duct

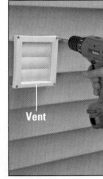

Vent

Cut vinyl with a fine-toothed handsaw, hole saw, or by repeated scoring with a utility knife. In some cases you may have to purchase a tool that "unzips" one course of siding from the next. For double protection, install the duct and carefully caulk around it. Then install the vent with galvanized screws and caulk around the duct and the vent housing.

ROOF FAN

If it is not possible to install a gable fan *(pages 88–89)*, a roof fan is the next best choice. Wiring is simple. The hard part is slipping it under shingles so the roof will not leak. Follow the manufacturer's instructions for exactly how to cut the hole and attach the fan. If the roof already has a turbine or other vent, you may be able to remove it and install a roof fan with little or no cutting.

Many roof fans have humidistats, which measure humidity, as well as thermostats. They rid the attic of excess moisture, which can damage insulation even if the attic is not hot.

PRESTART CHECKLIST

☐ **TIME**
About five hours to cut a hole in the roof, install the fan, and run cable inside an attic

☐ **TOOLS**
Voltage tester, drill, bit, reciprocating or saber saw, pry bar, utility and putty knives, screwdriver, strippers, longnose pliers, lineman's pliers

☐ **SKILLS**
Cutting roofing; stripping, splicing, connecting wires

☐ **PREP**
Find power source and make sure that the fan will not overload the circuit *(pages 24–25, 42–43)*

☐ **MATERIALS**
Roof fan, cable, roofing nails, roofing cement, screws, wire nuts, cable clamps, electrician's tape

1 Drill a locator hole from the inside of the attic to ensure that you will not cut through a joist. Mark the roof with the manufacturer's template and cut the hole with a saber saw or reciprocating saw.

2 You may need to cut back some shingles. Slide the fan into place so that the top half of its flange is covered with shingles.

3 Drive roofing nails and cover them with roofing cement. Use roofing cement to seal down the roofing above and beside the vent. Wire the fan as you would a gable fan *(page 89)*.

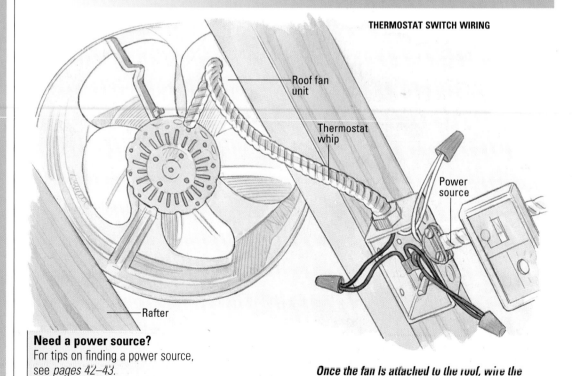

THERMOSTAT SWITCH WIRING

Need a power source?
For tips on finding a power source, see *pages 42–43*.

Once the fan is attached to the roof, wire the fan's thermostat directly to a power source.

RANGE HOOD

A range hood clears the air over a cooking surface. It may also provide illumination. Usually it is attached to the underside of a cabinet, about 30 inches above the range. The bottom of the hood should be about 24 inches above the range.

The larger a range hood's "cfm" rating (the cubic feet per minute of air it draws), the greater its capacity to expel smoke, heat, and odors.

If the ducts will have to travel more than a few feet or make several turns to reach the outside, a range hood will not be very effective. Consider purchasing a ductless unit, which runs air through a filter and sends it back into the kitchen.

To replace a range hood, **shut off power** and remove the existing hood. Take the hood with you when you buy a new one to make sure the duct work will line up.

PRESTART CHECKLIST

☐ **TIME**
About six hours to cut holes, run cable, and install ductwork and a range hood (not including cutting a pathway for the cable and patching walls)

☐ **TOOLS**
Voltage tester, drill, long bit, perhaps a masonry bit and cold chisel, saw, hammer, fish tape, longnose pliers, screwdriver, strippers, lineman's pliers

☐ **SKILLS**
Stripping, splicing, and connecting wires to terminals; running cable through walls; cutting holes in walls

☐ **PREP**
Find power source and make sure the range hood will not overload the circuit (pages 24–25, 42–43). Spread a drop cloth on the floor below.

☐ **MATERIALS**
Range hood, cable and clamps, ducts, duct tape, sheet metal screws, wall cap, caulk, wire nuts, electrician's tape

Drywall saw

1 Remove the range hood electrical cover and punch out the knockouts for the duct and for the electrical connection. Hold the hood in position and mark the wall for two holes. Cut a hole in the wall (page 48) for the duct.

Long bit for locator holes

2 If necessary, drill a hole for the cable. Equip a drill with a long bit and drill locator holes through to the outside of the house.

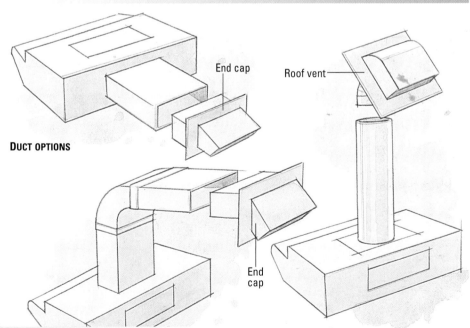

End cap

Roof vent

DUCT OPTIONS

End cap

A standard range hood pulls only about 3 amps (360 watts) so it is often possible to connect it to a kitchen's receptacle circuit.

Run ductwork in the most direct route possible. If you cannot go straight out the wall, route the ducts up through cabinets and then either out the roof or out the wall.

RANGE HOOD (continued)

Locator holes

Saber saw

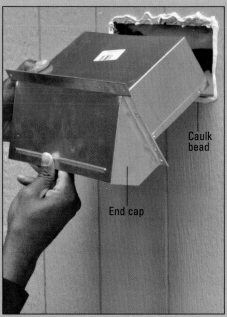

Caulk bead

End cap

3 Mark the cutout by connecting the locator holes. Check to see that the hole will be the right size for your duct. Cut through siding using a saber saw, reciprocating saw, or circular saw.

4 Shut off power to the circuit. Connect cable to a power source *(pages 42–43)* and run it up through the cable hole. You may use the cutout for the duct to help access and handle the cable, but make sure the cable will not be in the way of the duct.

5 Measure from the outside to the inside wall and cut a piece of duct to fit. Attach the duct to the end cap. Apply a bead of caulk around the hole on the outside and slide the duct and cap through the wall. Attach the cap with screws.

For vent hole in cabinet

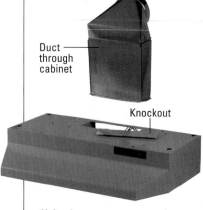

Duct through cabinet

Knockout

If the duct must run upward, remove the knockout on top of the hood and install the damper unit. Cut cabinets carefully to make room for the duct.

Bending sheet metal

To join a duct to a range hood (left) you may have to cut the duct to size and bend your own flange. For a straight, neat angle, score the bend with the end of screwdriver, clamp on two 1×2s as shown above, and bend the flange.

Cutting and attaching to a masonry wall

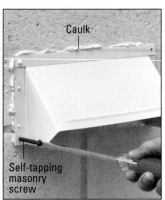

Caulk

Self-tapping masonry screw

Use a masonry bit to drill the locator holes (Step 2). To cut through brick, drill holes every inch or two, then chip away with a hammer and cold chisel. An older home may have two thicknesses of brick.

Purchase masonry screws along with a masonry bit of the appropriate size for the screws. Drill a pilot hole and drive the masonry screw into the block.

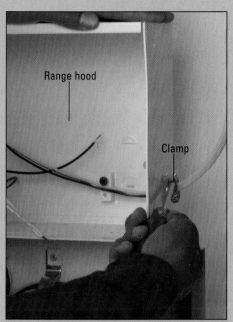

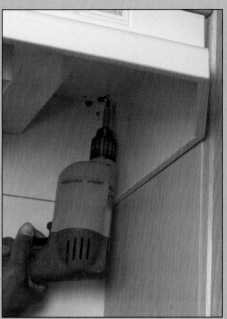

6 Stuff the cavity around the duct with insulation. Strip and clamp cable to the range hood.

7 Slip the range hood into place so the duct fits snugly over the hood's damper unit. Attach the hood with screws driven up into the cabinet above and/or into the wall studs.

8 Connect the grounds, including the pigtail to the hood housing. Splice the hood's lead wires to the house wires. Reattach the electrical cover.

WHAT IF...
A stud is in the way?

If a stud is in the way of the most direct route for the duct, try working around it with flexible ductwork. Another option is to cut a wall opening large enough to install a header but small enough that it will be covered by the range hood and the cabinet above it. Cut the stud and install a header made of doubled 2×4s sandwiching ½-inch plywood.

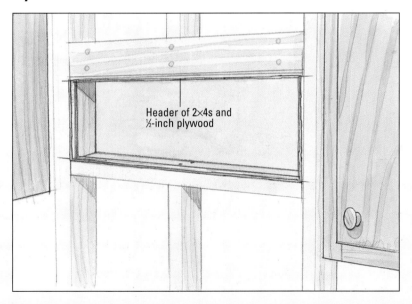

Header of 2×4s and ½-inch plywood

STANLEY PRO TIP

Range hood maintenance and use

■ Check that the damper flap moves freely so air can move out only when the fan is blowing.
■ Remove the filter every few months and clean or replace it.
■ Clean the underside of the hood regularly. Built-up grease poses a fire hazard.
■ When cooking with high heat, turn on the fan to cool the air and reduce the risk of a grease fire.

BATH VENT FAN

Many bathroom fans do little more than make noise, either because they are too weak or because their ductwork does not permit free movement of air. Usually venting is the culprit. Plan for a vent duct that is as short as possible and that makes as few turns as possible *(page 95)*.

In addition to a vent fan, a bathroom unit may have a light, night-light, and/or a heater unit. Because a heater uses much more power than a light and fan, it may need to be on its own circuit.

A fan-only unit or a light and fan that come on at the same time requires only two-cable wiring. The more features you want to control separately, the more complicated the wiring becomes. To replace an existing fan, check the wiring; you may need to replace two-wire cable with three-wire cable or even two cables.

PRESTART CHECKLIST

☐ **TIME**
About seven hours to install ducting, a fan, and a switch (not including cutting a pathway for the cable and patching walls)

☐ **TOOLS**
Voltage tester, pry bar, drill, saw, hammer, nonconductive ladder, fish tape, screwdriver, strippers, longnose pliers, lineman's pliers

☐ **SKILLS**
Cutting through siding or roofing; stripping, splicing, and connecting wires; installing boxes; running cable

☐ **PREP**
Find the shortest path for the ductwork. Find power source and make sure that the new lights will not overload the circuit *(pages 24–25, 42–43)*. Spread a drop cloth on the floor below.

☐ **MATERIALS**
Vent fan, switch, ductwork, duct tape, sheet metal screws, cable, clamps, switch box, wire nuts, electrician's tape

A. Install the vent fan housing

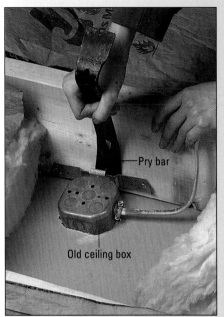
Old ceiling box / Pry bar

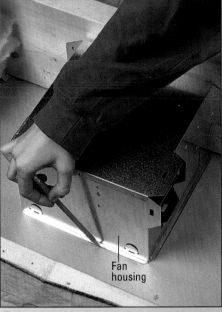
Fan housing

1 To replace an existing ceiling light with a fan/light, **shut off power to the circuit.** Remove the light and pry out the ceiling box. If you cannot work from above, cut carefully around the box before prying. You may need to cut through mounting nails.

2 Disassemble the new fixture and use the housing as a template to mark for the opening. The fan must be securely mounted; if there is no joist to attach it to, install blocking nailed to nearby joists.

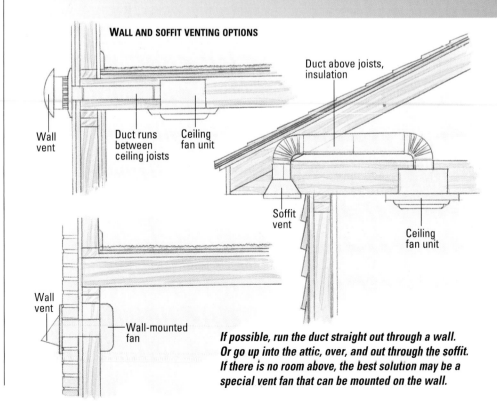

WALL AND SOFFIT VENTING OPTIONS

Wall vent

Duct runs between ceiling joists

Ceiling fan unit

Duct above joists, insulation

Soffit vent

Ceiling fan unit

Wall vent

Wall-mounted fan

If possible, run the duct straight out through a wall. Or go up into the attic, over, and out through the soffit. If there is no room above, the best solution may be a special vent fan that can be mounted on the wall.

Blocking

Drywall saw

3 If necessary, install blocking to keep the insulation away from the fan. Cut the hole with a drywall saw or reciprocating saw. If the ceiling is plaster, drill locator holes at the four corners and cut the opening from below.

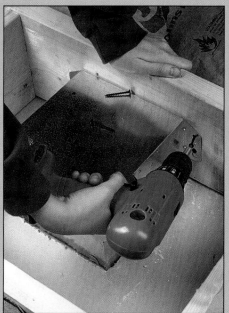

4 If necessary, run new cable from the switch to the box *(pages 50–53)*. (The fan pictured above has separate controls for fan and light and requires one three-wire cable.) Screw the fan to a framing member.

Locator hole

Saber saw

5 For the wall vent, drill a locator hole from the inside through the outside wall. Outside, cut a hole for the duct.

WHAT IF...
You must work from below?

If there is no access to an attic space above, cut the hole next to a joist. If the duct can run parallel to a joist and the outside wall is not too far away, use a long bit to drill the locator hole.

STANLEY PRO TIP

Ducts should be short, wide, and smooth

The shorter, smoother, and wider the ductwork, the more freely air can move through it. Most ductwork for bathroom fans is 4 inches in diameter; don't use anything smaller. Solid ducting is the smoothest and most efficient, but it may be difficult to install in tight places. All-metal flexible duct is bendable and fairly smooth. Plastic-and-wire ducting is the easiest to install but is the least efficient.

At every joint, use sheet metal screws or clamps to make tight connections, then cover the joint completely with professional-quality duct tape.

Venting through the roof

Roof jack

To install a roof jack *(page 96)*, follow the manufacturer's instructions exactly to ensure that the jack will not leak. First cut through the roof, then cut back shingles. Install the jack and cover its top half with shingles. Cover all nails with roofing cement *(page 90)*.

A. Install the vent fan housing (continued)

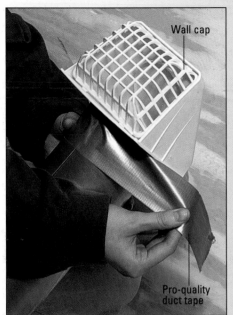

Wall cap

Pro-quality duct tape

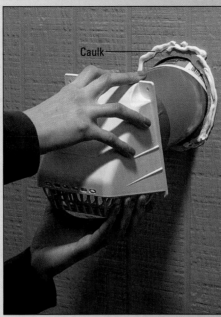

Caulk

Clamp

6 Measure from the outside to the fan. Attach a piece of solid duct to the wall cap so it is long enough to reach the fan or as close as possible. Fit the duct to the cap, drill pilot holes, and drive sheet-metal screws to hold. Then cover the joint with professional-quality duct tape.

7 Run a bead of caulk around the exterior hole. Slide the duct through the hole and fasten the wall cap to the wall with screws.

8 Fill any gap between duct and fan with another piece of solid duct or with flexible metal ducting. At each joint, attach clamps and wrap with duct tape.

ROOF VENT

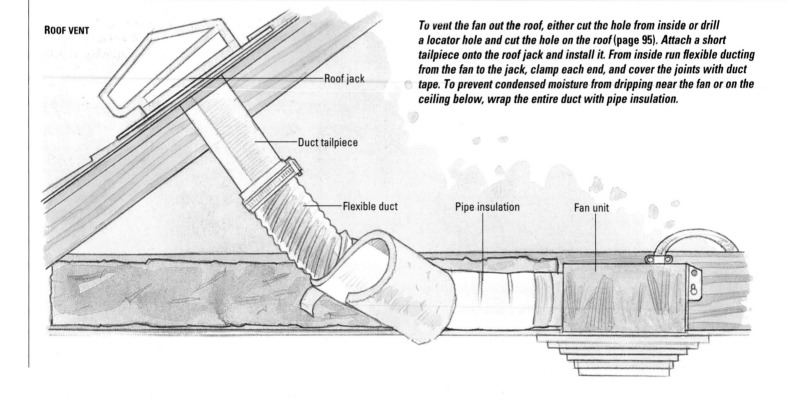

Roof jack

Duct tailpiece

Flexible duct

Pipe insulation

Fan unit

To vent the fan out the roof, either cut the hole from inside or drill a locator hole and cut the hole on the roof (page 95). Attach a short tailpiece onto the roof jack and install it. From inside run flexible ducting from the fan to the jack, clamp each end, and cover the joints with duct tape. To prevent condensed moisture from dripping near the fan or on the ceiling below, wrap the entire duct with pipe insulation.

B. Wire the fan

3-wire cable

Power source

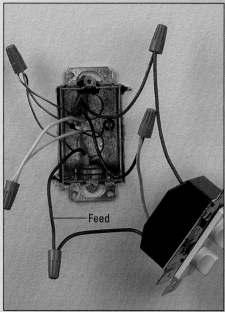

Feed

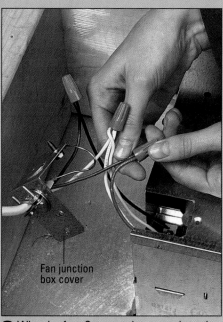

Fan junction box cover

1 If necessary, run the correct cable or cables to the switch box. As shown above, power enters the switch box. If power enters the fan, consult the manufacturer's instructions.

2 To wire a fan/light switch, connect the grounds and splice the white wires. Connect the red and black wires from the fan to the fan and light terminals. Connect the feed wire to the remaining terminal.

3 Wire the fan. Connect the grounds and splice the white wires. Splice the black wire to the black fan lead and the red wire to the colored lead. Attach the junction box cover. In the bathroom, install the light and the fixture canopy.

Timer switch for a fan with a heater

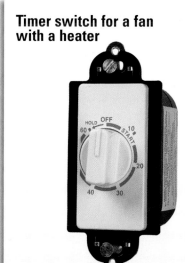

To avoid wasting energy and creating a hazardous situation by leaving on the fan heater, install a timer switch (above) along with a two-function switch for the fan and light. To do so, install a double-gang box.

WIRING A MULTIPURPOSE UNIT

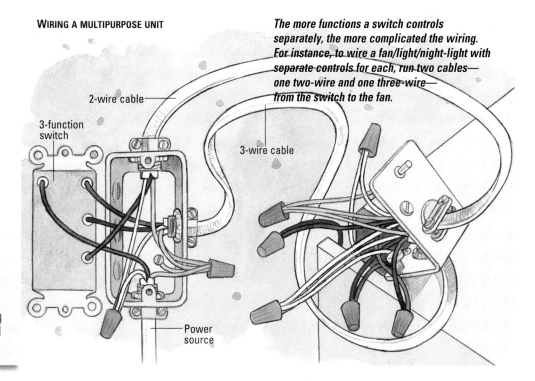

2-wire cable

3-function switch

3-wire cable

Power source

The more functions a switch controls separately, the more complicated the wiring. For instance, to wire a fan/light/night-light with separate controls for each, run two cables—one two-wire and one three-wire—from the switch to the fan.

INSTALLING OUTDOOR WIRING

Low-voltage outdoor lights are inexpensive and easy to install. Kits typically include five or more lights, cable, and a transformer/timer. Some lights are mounted on stakes poked into the ground; others can be attached to posts. The cable runs in a shallow trench or sits on top of the ground and is covered with mulch; the transformer/timer simply plugs into a standard receptacle.

Low-voltage lights are bright enough to light a path, accent foliage, or provide muted lighting for an outdoor dining area. For brighter illumination, or to install an outdoor receptacle, standard 120-volt wiring is needed.

Choosing lights and switches

The first step in an outdoor wiring project is to decide where to put lights and receptacles. *Pages 100–101* give some ideas. Gather more tips by consulting with neighbors and salespeople. For switches, there are four basic options: standard switches, timers, motion-sensor switches, and photo cells, which turn lights on at dusk and off at dawn. Motion-sensors and photo cells are often built into outdoor light fixtures such as flood lights, but they can also be installed as switches that control several lights.

If you already have an outdoor receptacle, and if its circuit will not be overloaded when you add new service *(pages 24–25)*, grab power there. If this is not possible, *see pages 102–103* for moving power outdoors. *Pages 104–107* show how to run lines and install fixtures.

Meeting code

A permit is required for running standard-voltage cable outdoors. Local codes vary considerably, so have plans approved by your building department. Be clear on what sort of cable and/or conduit is required, how deep underground it must be buried, and what type of weathertight connections and fixtures are required. Always contact utilities for cable and pipe locations before digging.

Exterior lights and outlets add safety and enhance a home's appearance.

CHAPTER PREVIEW

Planning outdoor lighting
page 100

Extending power outdoors
page 102

Running outdoor cable
page 104

Outdoor fixtures
page 106

Stripping UF cable: Underground feed (UF) cable is more difficult to strip than standard NM, because the sheathing and insulation are molded together. Cut carefully with a knife to strip the sheathing and use standard strippers to strip insulation.

The wiring for typical outdoor installations is simple. Burying cable and protecting fixtures from damage is the difficult part. You'll need not only standard wiring tools, but also layout materials, a shovel for trenching, and possibly a clamshell digger for postholes.

PLANNING OUTDOOR LIGHTING

Outdoor lights not only provide a pleasant setting for outdoor activities, highlight interesting features of a yard or patio, and light a pathway, they can make your home safer by deterring criminals. The most challenging stage of an outdoor lighting project is running cable from a power source inside your home and making sure the outdoor cable is protected. Otherwise, the wiring is straightforward.

A system for all purposes

Aim for flexibility when choosing the type and number of outdoor lights and switches. For instance, use low-voltage lights controlled by a timer or photo cell to provide inexpensive lighting all night long.

For security and to light pathways when you come home at night, add bright standard-voltage lights that are controlled by motion sensors.

For a dramatic effect, point accent lights at trees or foliage and control them with a standard switch or a timer. To provide lighting for outdoor dining or parties, hang decorative standard-voltage lights overhead and control them with a dimmer switch.

Choosing lights

Make scale drawings of your property, including foliage, sidewalks, and paths. Pencil in the type of lighting you want in various areas.

Bring the drawing to a home center or lighting store and think through the possibilities. You'll find a wide selection of lights that poke into the ground, mount on posts, attach to siding, or hang overhead. Mix and match fixtures, choosing from the many available options *(page 106)*.

Floodlights provide plenty of illumination for a small cost so you may be tempted to light up your entire yard with them. However, while floods are excellent for security purposes, most people find them too glaring for dining and entertaining.

Cable and conduit

Outdoor rooms are casual so exposed conduit may not be considered unsightly. Plastic (PVC) conduit is pretty rugged, but metal conduit is more resistant to hard knocks. Consider installing metal wherever it might get bumped—for example, by a lawn mower. See *pages 38–40* for instructions on running plastic and metal conduit. Codes prohibit exposed cable outdoors, because it can be easily damaged.

Always use approved UF cable for outside wiring. *Pages 104–105* show how to hide it underground. Though resistant to moisture, UF cable is vulnerable to damage from a shovel or hammer, so protect it well. When installing an eaves or porch light, run standard cable through the attic or through a wall *(pages 48–53)*. When installing a post light on top of a 4×4, one option is to run the cable through a groove in the post, then cover the groove with a 1×2.

Easy lights

In addition to permanent lights, you can also put up decorative lanterns or even a string of holiday lights, which can be quickly added and easily moved. Miniature lights strung from trees render a magical feeling all year long. Exterior-rated rope lights can be hung under railings or stair treads, or over doorways. If stretched taut they have a high-tech look; draped in casual loops, they make for a party atmosphere.

Holiday lighting

If you're one of those people who love outdoor holiday decorations, don't assume that you can just plug all those colored lights and illuminated reindeer into any old receptacle. Typically, these setups use lots of low-wattage bulbs. They can quickly add up to a circuit overload, especially if the circuit runs to a living or family room where a home entertainment system is plugged in.

Plan for holiday lights as you would any electrical installation. Add up the wattages of all the bulbs and check to see that you won't overload a circuit. You may need to plug half the lights into a receptacle on one circuit and the other half into a receptacle that's on another circuit. Elaborate displays may call for a new circuit.

Shedding light on home security

Even the most brazen thief prefers the cover of darkness. By adding a combination of these security features you can add an inexpensive layer of defense against home invasion.
■ The brighter the light, the greater the deterrent. Bright lights triggered by motion detectors can have a startling effect. However, set your detector so it is not tripped by innocent dog walkers.
■ Surprise potential intruders with motion-sensor lights that turn on when they approach.

■ Make sure all pathways—both front and back—are illumined.
■ Have at least two lights pointed at each area of your lot, in case a bulb burns out.
■ Place some lights out of easy reach; some thieves like to unscrew or break bulbs. High-placed porch lights or eaves lights fit the bill.
■ An indoor light controlled by a motion sensor provides the greatest surprise, making it look like someone is home.

SAFETY FIRST
Check before you dig

Hidden under your lawn may be several utility lines—the main water supply, the gas or propane line, or even an underground electrical line. Find out where all four lines—water, gas, electricity, and telephone—run, as well as how deep they are buried, before you start digging trenches or postholes in the yard. Utility companies often provide one number to call for locating all lines.

Pole lamp

Floodlight with
photocell

Bulkhead
lamp

GFCI
receptacle

Riser light

Low-voltage
up lights

Low-voltage
pathway lighting

When lighting a yard, first make sure all pathways are lit and take care
of security concerns (page 100). Then turn your attention to lights that
enhance your yard's appearance at night. Upward-shining lights
dramatically highlight brushes and trees. Smaller lights can spotlight
lower plantings or shine from inside a hedge or flower bed. Lights that
swivel can be adjusted as foliage grows and seasons change. With its
mixture of low-voltage and standard-voltage lights, this outdoor space
can brighten an evening get-together and provide enough light for safety.

EXTENDING POWER OUTDOORS

Position an outdoor receptacle where it will stay dry—at least 16 inches above the ground—and out of harm's way. An in-use cover (Step 5) increases protection from the weather. A simple wooden box built around it shields it from bumps by the lawn mower or kids at play. Outdoor receptacles must be GFCI-protected. Check local codes for the types of cable, conduit, and boxes approved for your home.

The quickest way to extend power outdoors is to install a receptacle back-to-back with one inside the house *(page 103)*. Another simple solution is to drill through the wall from a basement or crawlspace and attach a receptacle on the side of a house using an extension ring *(Steps 1 and 2)*.

PRESTART CHECKLIST

☐ **TIME**
About two hours to install a new outdoor receptacle with extension ring and in-use cover (not including cutting a pathway for the cable, patching walls)

☐ **TOOLS**
Voltage tester, screwdriver, hammer, drill, saw, lineman's pliers, longnose pliers, strippers

☐ **SKILLS**
Stripping, splicing, and connecting wires to terminals; installing boxes, running cable through walls and ceilings

☐ **PREP**
Make sure that the new service will not overload the circuit *(pages 24–25)*

☐ **MATERIALS**
GFCI receptacle, outdoor box with extension ring and in-use cover, remodel box, cable, conduit and fittings, wire nuts, electrician's tape

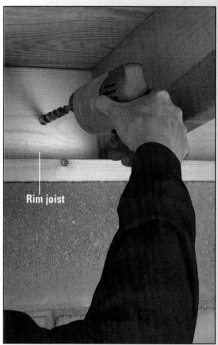

Rim joist

1 Find the easiest path for cable to reach an outside wall, perhaps through a basement or crawlspace. Use a long drill bit to drill a locator hole. If the location is inconvenient or does not satisfy codes, install an LB fitting *(page 103)* rather than a receptacle to run power elsewhere.

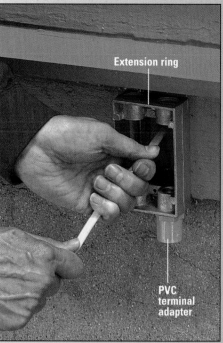

Extension ring

PVC terminal adapter

2 Cut a hole for a remodel box using a reciprocating saw or keyhole saw. If the exterior is masonry, see *page 92*. Run cable through the hole and into a remodel box. Install the box and add an extension ring and a terminal adapter if using PVC (shown).

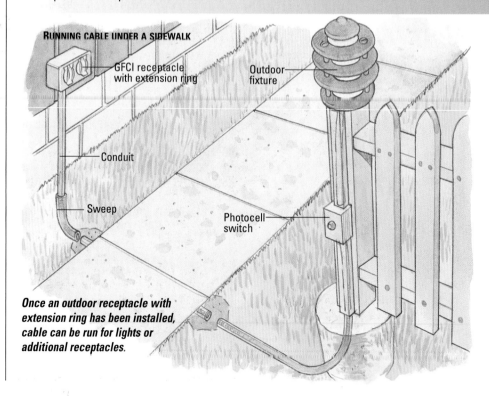

RUNNING CABLE UNDER A SIDEWALK

GFCI receptacle with extension ring

Outdoor fixture

Conduit

Sweep

Photocell switch

Once an outdoor receptacle with extension ring has been installed, cable can be run for lights or additional receptacles.

3 Beneath the box, dig a trench deep enough to satisfy local codes *(page 104)*. **Call before you dig.** Using PVC or rigid metal conduit, attach a length of pipe to a sweep. Cut the pipe to fit, attach it, and anchor the conduit with straps.

4 **Shut off power to the circuit.** Connect the black and white wires to the LINE terminals of a GFCI receptacle. After you run cable for the new service *(pages 104–105)*, connect those wires to the LOAD terminals. This way, all the new service will be GFCI-protected. Connect to the power source.

5 Install an in-use cover, which protects the receptacle from moisture even when a cord is plugged in.

Metal conduit

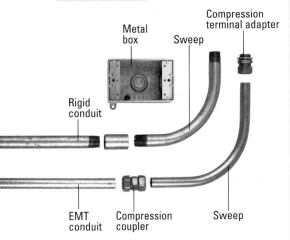

Metal conduit must be installed so it is watertight. Use rigid conduit with threaded fittings or EMT conduit with compression fittings.

Back-to-back wiring

One way to bring power outdoors is with back-to-back receptacles. **Shut off power,** pull out an indoor receptacle, and drill a locator hole through the wall to the outside.

WHAT IF…
You don't need a receptacle?

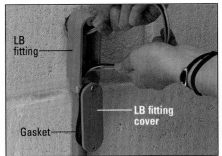

To make the transition from indoor to outdoor wiring, use an LB fitting. Essentially a watertight pulling elbow, it is ideal for connecting to conduit.

Ground fault circuit interrupter (GFCI)
A GFCI receptacle isn't necessary if the circuit is protected with a GFCI breaker or if the new line taps into a GFCI receptacle.

RUNNING OUTDOOR CABLE

While some building departments require underground wiring to run through metal or plastic conduit, most codes call for conduit only where the wiring is exposed or buried in a shallow trench. (Even when conduit is watertight, condensation can moisten underground wiring. UF cable offers the only real protection against water damage.)

Before you start to dig, ask your utility companies to mark the locations of water, gas, electric, or phone lines. Most have a toll-free number available.

A square-bladed spade will handle short runs. If you need to dig more than 50 feet of trenches, consider renting a powered trench digger.

Consult local building codes carefully. For instance, some codes allow for a shallower trench if the cable or conduit is covered with a 2×6 pressure-treated plank.

PRESTART CHECKLIST

☐ **TIME**
Once power is brought outside *(pages 102–103)*, about a day to dig trenches, run 60 feet of cable, and install several lights *(pages 106–107)*

☐ **TOOLS**
Shovel, posthole digger, hammer, drill, fish tape, pliers, garden hose or sledge hammer

☐ **SKILLS**
Laying out and digging trenches, fishing cable through conduit

☐ **PREP**
Install a receptacle or LB fitting bringing power to the outside and check that the new service will not overload the circuit *(pages 24–25)*. Call utility company to mark lines.

☐ **MATERIALS**
Conduit and fittings, conduit clamps, stakes, string line

1 **After the utility companies have marked the location of any underground lines,** plan a route that stays several feet away from them. Use string lines and stakes to indicate the path for the underground cable.

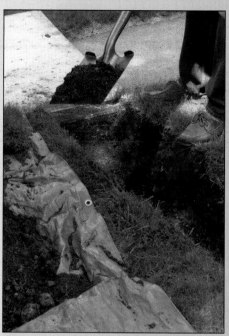

2 Cut the sod carefully with a square-bladed shovel so you can replace it later. Dig a trench deep enough to satisfy local codes. If you encounter a large root or rock, consider running the cable under it.

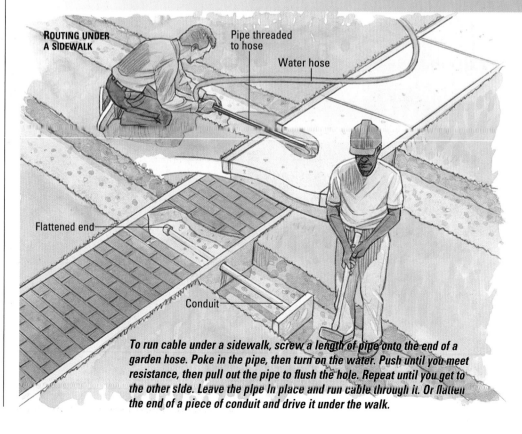

To run cable under a sidewalk, screw a length of pipe onto the end of a garden hose. Poke in the pipe, then turn on the water. Push until you meet resistance, then pull out the pipe to flush the hole. Repeat until you get to the other side. Leave the pipe in place and run cable through it. Or flatten the end of a piece of conduit and drive it under the walk.

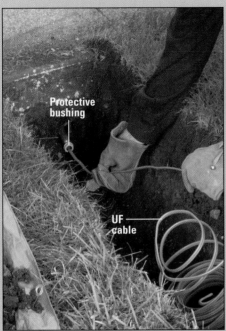

3 Run metal conduit under the sidewalk (use one of the methods shown on *page 104*). and attach a protective bushing to each end. Push the UF cable through the conduit.

4 Unroll the cable carefully to avoid kinks. Have a helper feed it through the conduit as you thread it through the trenches and conduit all the way to the power source.

5 When running cable to a lamp post, be sure to set the post so its access hole faces the trench (see *page 106* for more on setting fixtures). Carefully push the cable into the access hole and up the body of the post.

Bushing at end of conduit

Codes typically require a bushing at the end of the conduit to protect the cable sheathing. This is especially important when using metal conduit, which can easily slice through plastic sheathing.

Sink that cable
Local codes specify how deep cable or conduit must be buried. Encase it in conduit wherever it is less than the required depth.

Running wires through metal conduit

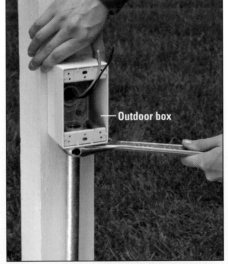

If codes call for a continuous run of metal conduit, purchase watertight boxes and fittings. Take care to tighten each fitting; one bad connection will result in wet wires.

Run wire through the conduit using a fish tape, as shown on *page 41*.

OUTDOOR FIXTURES

Home centers carry a variety of lights designed for outdoor use. Fixtures that use standard incandescent bulbs provide plenty of light for most residential purposes. Outdoor fluorescent fixtures may save energy costs but are usually more effective in an enclosed space like a garage (some may not work in cold weather). For the brightest illumination, use mercury vapor or halide fixtures.

Whatever fixture you install, pay special attention to its gasket. When you attach the cover, the gasket should be sandwiched tightly to seal out all moisture.

These two pages show how to set posts in concrete. In many areas, filling the hole around the post with well-tamped soil is considered just as strong.

Some lights come with cylindrical metal posts. Install these in much the same way as the post light shown here.

PRESTART CHECKLIST

☐ **TIME**
Once cable is run, about four hours to install a post and light; less time for other types of lights

☐ **TOOLS**
A posthole digger, post level, screwdriver, hammer, drill, chisel, strippers, longnose pliers, lineman's pliers

☐ **SKILLS**
Running cable outdoors, stripping, splicing, connecting wires to terminals

☐ **PREP**
Run cable and connect it to a circuit that will not be overloaded by the new service

☐ **MATERIALS**
An outdoor fixture, conduit, post, wire nuts, electrician's tape, concrete mix

1 **Don't start digging until the utility company has marked lines.** Plan locations of fixtures and trenches to avoid utility lines. Dig a trench to the fixture location *(pages 104–105)*. Use a clamshell digger to bore a hole at least 36 inches deep (including the depth of the trench).

2 Set the post in the hole. Plumb it with a level and brace it firmly with 1×4s. Fill the hole with concrete, leave the braces in place, and allow a day or so for the concrete to cure.

Gentle lighting options

Outdoor lights run the gamut from familiar low-voltage tier lights and undereaves floodlights to light-equipped outdoor-rated ceiling fans. For a subtle effect, consider the following options: Low-voltage **post lights** mount to the top of a 4×4 post, linking into a low-voltage run for their power.

Some **rope lights** are designed for outdoor use. Staple them to the underside of railings or decking overhangs or drape them from above.

For deck lighting without glare use low-profile **edge lights** or **surface lights** to illumine traffic areas and stairways or simply to add an accent.

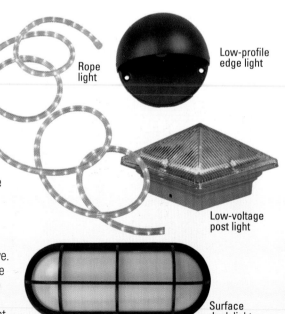

Rope light

Low-profile edge light

Low-voltage post light

Surface deck light

3 After the concrete has cured, attach the conduit and sweep to the box and fasten the box to the post. Attach a bushing to the sweep *(page 105)*.

4 Strip about 8 inches of sheathing from the UF cable and push the wires up through the conduit to the box. Run the cable to the power source, removing any kinks and laying the cable flat in the trench. Connect a GFCI receptacle *(page 59)* to the cable wires.

5 Fold in the wires and fasten the receptacle to the box. Place the gasket around the receptacle and fasten the outdoor receptacle cover.

Receptacle and post light

Bore a channel down from the top of the post to the level of the box using a ¾-inch bit. Drill from the side to connect the hole. Run cable through the channel and through a punch-out hole in the back of the box.

Undereaves light

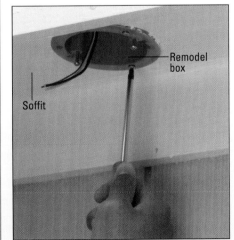

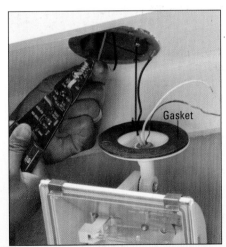

1 To install a light that hangs under the eaves, cut a hole for a round remodel box in the soffit. Run cable to the hole and clamp it to the box. Install the box.

2 Strip and splice the wires to the fixture's leads and attach the fixture. Check the gasket to make sure it is seated evenly and securely around the box to seal out water.

COMPLETING NEW CIRCUITS

Wiring an electrical appliance such as a dishwasher, disposer, or electric water heater is often the easiest part of a job—moving the unit in and connecting the plumbing will take most of your time. This chapter shows how to install many of the most common types of major household appliances. It also walks you through how to run a new circuit if the appliance requires it.

Whenever you add a new appliance or upgrade an old one, check the wattage ratings to make sure you will not overload a circuit *(pages 24-25)*. With an upgrade, you may be surprised to find that your new appliance actually *reduces* the load. The reason is many new appliances—refrigerator, toaster, microwave, dishwasher, water heater, for instance—use less power than the older models they replace.

Installing a new circuit
Some new appliances—a spa, baseboard heater, or a window air-conditioner—may need a new circuit. As long as your service panel has room for a new circuit, the wiring is not difficult. Running the cable will consume most of your time. *Pages 112–113* show how.

Before adding a new circuit, consult *pages 26–27* to make sure that your basic electrical service can handle the extra load. If not, have an electrician install a new service panel.

Adding a subpanel
If the service panel does not have enough room for a new circuit, but your basic service can handle a new circuit, install a subpanel with room for a number of new circuits *(pages 114–115)*.

Some of these projects involve 240-volt circuits. The wiring is no more complicated than wiring for a 120-volt circuit, but the danger is much greater. A 240-volt shock can be very serious, even fatal. Work closely with a building inspector. **Double-check to see that power is shut off** before beginning any work. Call in a professional electrician to advise you, or have a pro do the work if you are at all unsure of yourself.

Here's how to add new circuits to a panel and connect permanently installed appliances.

CHAPTER PREVIEW

Hardwiring appliances
page 110

Hooking up a new circuit
page 112

Installing a subpanel
page 114

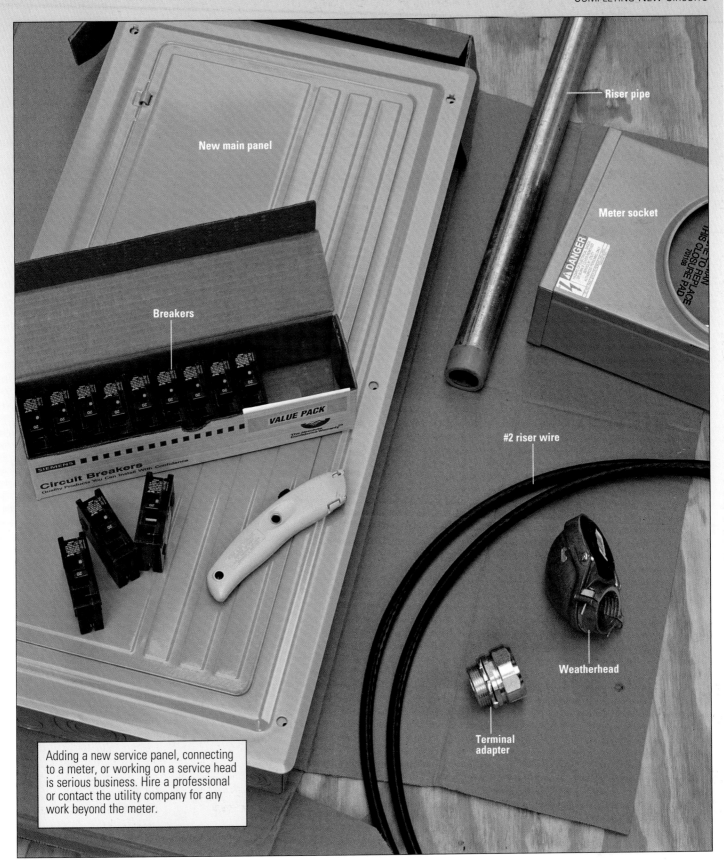

Riser pipe

New main panel

Meter socket

Breakers

VALUE PACK
The Memory
Confidence Warranty™

SIEMENS
Circuit Breakers
Quality Products You Can Install With Confidence

#2 riser wire

Weatherhead

Terminal
adapter

Adding a new service panel, connecting
to a meter, or working on a service head
is serious business. Hire a professional
or contact the utility company for any
work beyond the meter.

HARDWIRING APPLIANCES

Most 120-volt appliances simply plug into a standard receptacle. Some 240-volt appliances plug into special 240-volt receptacles *(pages 60–61)*. Other appliances—those that use 240 volts and are stationary—are "hardwired," meaning that cable is attached directly. Garbage disposers and dishwashers may be either plugged in or hardwired.

Shut off power to the circuit before installing any appliance. These pages give general directions for some typical installations. Consult with manufacturer's instructions before wiring—wire colors and cable connections may vary.

Appliance disconnects
If you shut off a circuit breaker to work on a 240-volt appliance, another person may mistakenly flip the breaker on while you are doing the wiring, creating a very dangerous situation. That is why building codes may require a hardwired appliance to have a "disconnect"—basically, an on/off switch. The disconnect must be positioned within sight of the appliance. An alternative is to install a circuit breaker with a lockout feature, which allows you to lock the breaker shut to prevent an accident.

PRESTART CHECKLIST

☐ **TIME**
About an hour to make most connections, once cable has been run

☐ **TOOLS**
Screwdriver, flashlight, strippers, lineman's pliers, longnose pliers

☐ **SKILLS**
Stripping, splicing, and connecting wires to terminals

☐ **PREP**
See that the new appliance will not overload the circuit *(pages 24–25)*. Remove the old appliance or run cable for a new appliance.

☐ **MATERIALS**
Appliance, wire nuts, electrician's tape

WIRING A DISPOSER

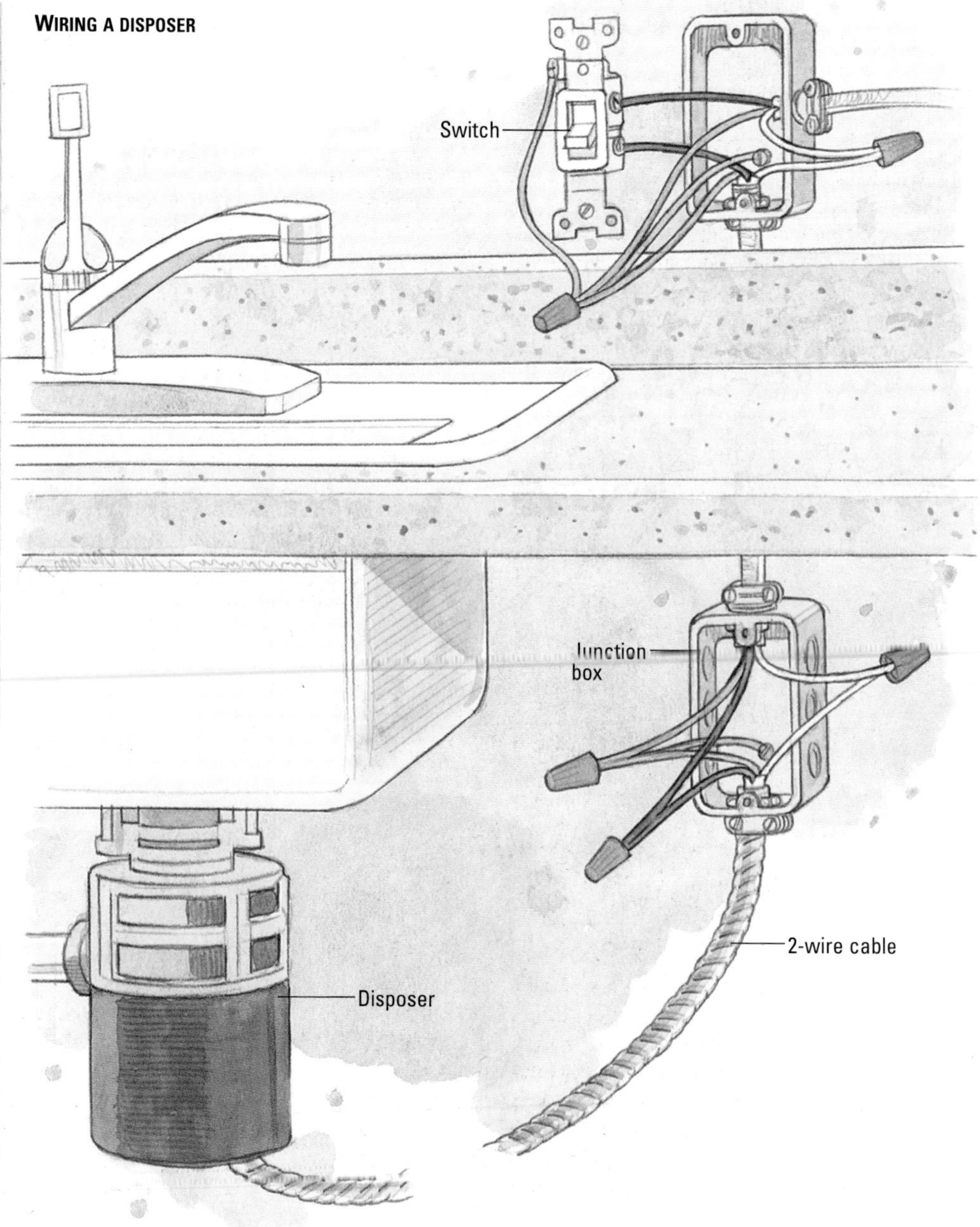

Switch

Junction box

2-wire cable

Disposer

Under the sink, a split and switched receptacle (pages 64–65) can provide an always-hot plug for a hot-water dispenser and a switched plug for the garbage disposer. Some codes may require the disposer to be hardwired, in which case a separate, switched junction box is needed (shown above).

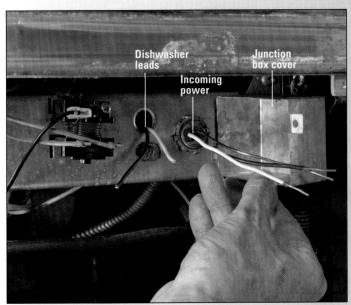

Dishwasher: Codes may require a dishwasher to be on a dedicated circuit. Some models plug into receptacles, but most are hardwired. Provide a cable that can reach to the front of the dishwasher. Slide the dishwasher into the space and make the plumbing connections. Open the dishwasher's junction box and splice wires to the dishwasher's leads. Replace the junction box cover.

Electric water heater: A water heater needs a dedicated 240-volt circuit. Check the unit's amperage rating and make sure the circuit can handle at least 120 percent of the rating. For most homes, a 30-amp circuit with 10/2 cable is sufficient. Because of the heat generated by the unit, use Greenfield or armored cable rather than NM cable. Remove the coverplate, splice the wires (note that a neutral is not required), and replace the coverplate.

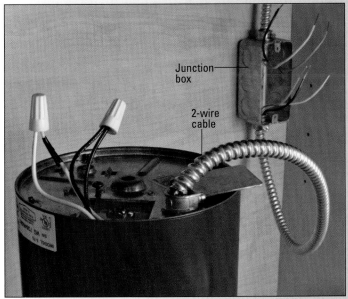

Garbage disposer: Garbage disposers are sold without cords, so they can be wired directly to cable (hardwiring) or to an appliance cord with a plug. Install armored cable (shown above) or buy a thick cord that can handle the disposer's amperage rating. Splice the wires to the disposer first. Install it in the sink. Then hard wire or plug it into a switched receptacle. A disposer should not be on a light circuit, or lights will dim when it starts.

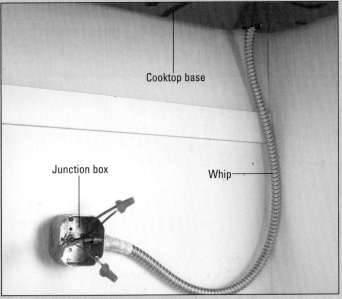

Electric cooktop: An electric cooktop or wall-mounted oven requires a 120/240-volt circuit—120 volts to power lights and timer, 240 volts for the heating elements. A cooktop and an oven can be wired to the same circuit. Run cable to a nearby junction box. An electric oven or cooktop usually has a short length of armored cable, called a "whip." Clamp the whip to the junction box; make the splices. Make sure the wire and breaker are big enough for both.

HOOKING UP A NEW CIRCUIT

Though it may sound complicated, connecting a new circuit is no more difficult than the other projects in this book. You'll spend most of your time running cable from the new service to the service panel *(pages 44–53)*.

Make sure that adding a new circuit will not overload your electrical system. Review *pages 26–27* and talk with an inspector or an electrician about your plans. If the service panel cannot accept another circuit, install a subpanel *(pages 114–115)*. If your system cannot accommodate a new circuit, have an electrician install a new service panel.

If there is an available slot for a new circuit breaker in your service panel, you can add a breaker there. If not, you may be able to replace a regular circuit breaker with a tandem breaker (below right).

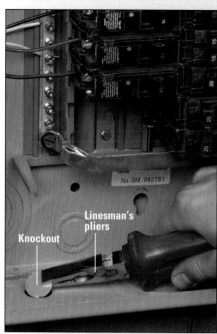

1 **Shut off the main breaker** and remove the panel's cover. Remove a knockout slug from the side of the cover.

Knockout

Linesman's pliers

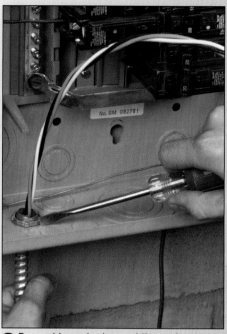

No. GM 082781

2 Run cable to the box, adding at least 2 feet extra for wiring work within the service panel. Strip enough sheathing from the cable to allow wires to travel most of the way around the panel. Slide the wires through the knockout hole and clamp the cable in place.

PRESTART CHECKLIST

☐ **TIME**
About two hours to make connections for a new circuit, once cable has been run

☐ **TOOLS**
Flashlight, hammer, screwdriver, strippers, lineman's pliers, longnose pliers, voltage tester

☐ **SKILLS**
Figuring loads on circuits, stripping sheathing and wire insulation, connecting wires to terminals

☐ **PREP**
Install boxes for the new service and run cable from the boxes to the service panel

☐ **MATERIALS**
New circuit breaker and cable

REFRESHER COURSE
When do you need a new circuit?

If new electrical service—lights, receptacles, or appliances—use so much wattage that they cannot be added to an existing circuit without overloading it, then a new circuit is called for. See *pages 24–25* for the calculations.

Extra protection
Install an Arc Fault Circuit Interrupter (AFCI) instead of a standard circuit breaker. It provides extra protection against fire due to frayed or overheated cords. They are now required for bedroom wiring.

Two for one with a tandem breaker

A tandem circuit breaker makes it possible to install two circuits in the space of one. Unlike double-power breakers *(page 113)*, tandem breakers can be switched off and on individually. Some panels do not allow for tandem breakers. Others allow only a certain number of tandems. Get an inspector's OK before you install a tandem.

3 Route the wires so they skirt the perimeter of the panel and stay far away from hot bus bars. Strip ½ inch of insulation from the neutral wire and connect it to the neutral bus bar. Connect the ground wire to the ground bus bar.

Ground bus bar

4 Bend the hot wire into position along the side of the panel, cut it to length, and strip ½ inch of insulation. Poke it into the breaker and tighten the setscrew.

Breaker

5 Slide one end of the breaker under the hot bus bar and push the breaker until it snaps in place and aligns with the surrounding breakers. Twist out a knockout slot in the service panel's cover and replace the cover.

WHAT IF...
There is only one neutral/ground bar?

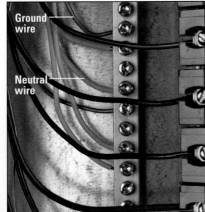

Ground wire

Neutral wire

Some service panels have separate bus bars for neutral and ground wires. Others have only one bar that serves both. Connect neutral and ground wires in any order.

STANLEY PRO TIP

Double-pole breakers

A double-pole breaker takes up twice the space of a single-pole breaker. You'll need it for 240-volt circuits and with two-circuit and split receptacles *(pages 62–63)*. Connect the ground and neutral wires to bus bars and connect the hot wires to the breaker.

GFCI breaker

A GFCI circuit breaker protects all the receptacles, lights, and appliances on its circuit. Connect both the hot and neutral wires to the breaker. Connect the breaker's white lead to the neutral bus bar.

INSTALLING A SUBPANEL

If the service panel does not have room for new circuit breakers and you cannot use tandem breakers (*page 112*), a subpanel may be the answer. Before installing one, consult with an inspector to make sure you will not overload your overall system.

A subpanel has separate bus bars for neutral and ground wires and typically has no main breaker. It may not be labeled "subpanel," but instead be labeled "lugs only." It may be a different brand than the main panel.

Have the inspector approve the subpanel, the feeder cable, and the feeder breaker (see *page 115*).

Shut off the main breaker in the service panel before you begin.

PRE-START CHECKLIST

☐ **TIME**
About four hours to install a subpanel with several new circuits, not including running cable for the new circuits

☐ **TOOLS**
Screwdriver, hammer, voltage tester, strippers, drill, lineman's pliers, longnose pliers

☐ **SKILLS**
Stripping sheathing and wires, connecting wires to terminals

☐ **PREP**
Run cables for the new circuits to the subpanel location. In the main service panel, make room for the double-pole feeder breaker.

☐ **MATERIALS**
Subpanel, mounting screws, approved feeder cable, staples or cable clamps, approved feeder breaker, breakers for the new circuits

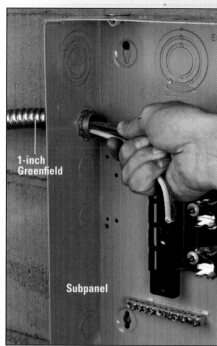

1 Mount the subpanel about a foot away from the main service panel. Determine how far the wires will have to travel in the subpanel, and pull wires (shown above) or add cable and strip sheathing accordingly. Remove a knockout slug, slide the wires through, and clamp the cable.

2 At the main service panel, plan the routes for the four wires: ground, neutral, and two hot wires (black and red). Strip the sheathing, remove a knockout slug, and clamp the cable. Route the neutral and ground wires carefully and connect them to the bus bar(s).

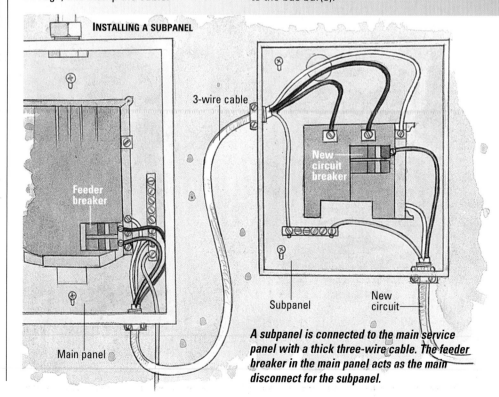

INSTALLING A SUBPANEL

A subpanel is connected to the main service panel with a thick three-wire cable. The feeder breaker in the main panel acts as the main disconnect for the subpanel.

3 Route, cut, and strip the red and black wires. Connect them to the feeder breaker. Snap the breaker into place.

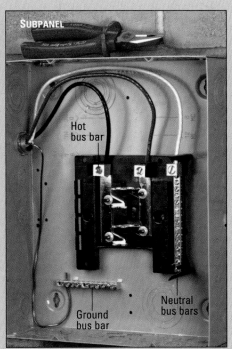

4 In the subpanel, route the feeder wires, cut and strip them, and connect to terminals. Connect the black and red wires to the hot bus bars, the neutral wire to the main neutral terminal, and the ground wire to the ground bar.

5 Run cable for new circuits into the subpanel and clamp the cable. For each circuit, route wires around the perimeter, connect the ground wire to the ground bar, the white wire to the neutral bar, and the hot wire to a circuit breaker.

Choosing a feeder breaker and cable

Buy a subpanel larger than you currently need so you'll be ready for future electrical improvements. The three parts—subpanel, feeder breaker, and cable—should be compatible in capacity.

To figure sizes, add up the wattages of all the new electrical users (see *pages 24-25*) and add 20 percent to take into account safe capacity. Then divide by 230 to get the amperage you will need.

For instance, if the new service will total 4,000 watts, add 20 percent (multiply by 1.2) to get 4,800; then divide 4,800 by 230 to get 20.8 amps. A subpanel supplying 30 amps of service will suffice.

As a general rule, to supply up to 5,700 watts of new power, install a 30-amp subpanel, a 30-amp feeder breaker, and 10/3 feeder cable. To supply up to 7,500 watts, install a 40-amp subpanel, a 40-amp feeder breaker, and 8/3 cable.

Cable with wires this thick may be difficult to find. If a home center does not carry it, call an electrical supply source.

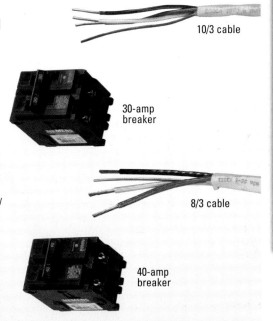

10/3 cable

30-amp breaker

8/3 cable

40-amp breaker

SAFETY FIRST
Keeping cable out of harm's way

Professional electricians take pride in the way they run wires in a service panel or subpanel. In a well-wired panel, wires are routed in neat paths around the perimeter, making it easy to tell which wire goes to which breaker. More importantly, orderly wires are less likely to brush against hot bus bars, which, if it happened, would create a serious fire hazard.

GLOSSARY

For terms not included here, or for more about those that are, refer to the index on pages 118–120.

Amp: Short for ampere, this is a measurement of the strength of electrical current flowing through a wire or appliance. An amperage rating tells the greatest amount of current a wire, device, or appliance can carry.

Armored cable: Flexible cable, containing two or more wires,with a protective metal sheathing. See *BX and MC cable.*

Box: A metal or plastic container with openings for cable. All electrical connections must be made inside a code-approved electrical box.

Bus bar: A long terminal inside a service panel. Circuit breakers or fuses connect to hot bus bars; neutral and ground wires connect to neutral and grounding bus bars. Some service panels have separate bus bars for neutral and ground wires (required in Canada), while others have only one neutral/ground bus bar.

BX cable: Armored cable containing insulated wires and no ground wire; the sheathing acts as the grounding path.

Cable: Two or more insulated wires wrapped in metal or plastic sheathing.

Circuit: Also called a branch circuit. Two or more wires carrying power from the service panel to devices, fixtures, and appliances and then back to the panel. Each circuit is protected by a circuit breaker or fuse in the service panel.

Circuit breaker: A protective device in a service panel that automatically shuts off power to its circuit when it senses a short circuit or overload.

Codes: Local regulations governing safe wiring practices. See National Electrical Code (NEC).

Common terminal: On a three-way switch, the darker-colored terminal (often marked COM) to which the wire supplying power is connected.

Common wire: In a three-way switch setup, the wire that brings power to the switch or to the fixture.

Conductor: A carrier of electricity—usually, a wire.

Conduit: Plastic or metal pipe through which wires run.

Continuity tester: A device that tells whether a circuit is capable of carrying electricity.

Cord: Two or more insulated stranded wires encased in a flexible plastic or cloth sheathing.

Current: The flow of electrons through a conductor.

Device: Usually an electrical receptacle or switch.

Duplex receptacle: The most common type of receptacle with two outlets.

Electrical Metallic Tubing (EMT): Thin rigid metal conduit suitable for residential use. Also called Thinwall.

End-line wiring: Also called switch-loop wiring. A method of wiring a switch, in which power runs to the fixture box. Compare through-switch wiring.

End-of-run: A receptacle at the end of a circuit.

Feed wire: The hot wire that brings power into a box.

Fixture: A light or fan that is permanently attached rather than being plugged into a receptacle.

Four-way switch: A switch used when a light is controlled by three or more switches.

Fuse: A safety device, located in a fuse box, which shuts off power when a circuit overloads.

Greenfield: Flexible metal conduit.

Ground: Wire or metal sheathing that provides an alternate path for current back to the service panel (and from there to a grounding rod sunk in the earth, or to a cold-water pipe). Grounding protects against shock in case of an electrical malfunction.

Ground Fault Circuit Interrupter (GFCI): A receptacle with a built-in safety feature, which shuts off when there is a risk of shock.

Hardwired: An appliance that is wired via cable directly into a box rather than having a cord that plugs into a receptacle.

Hot wire: The wire that carries power; it is either black or colored.

Junction box: An electrical box with no fixture or device attached; it is used to split a circuit into different branches.

Kilowatt (kW): One thousand watts.

Knockout: A round slug or a tab that can be punched out to allow room for a cable or circuit breaker.

LB fitting: A pulling elbow made for outdoor use.

Lead: A wire (usually stranded) connected to a fixture.

MC cable: Armored cable with a ground wire in addition to at least two insulated wires.

Middle-of-run: A receptacle located between the service panel and another receptacle. Wires continue from its box and on to one or more other receptacle boxes.

Multitester: A tool that measures voltage of various levels, tests for continuity, and performs other tests.

National Electrical Code (NEC): The standard set of electrical codes for the United States, updated every few years. Local codes sometimes vary from the NEC.

Neon tester: See Voltage tester.

Neutral wire: A wire, usually covered with white insulation, that carries power from the box back to the service panel. See also Hot wire and Ground.

Nonmetallic (NM) cable: Usually two or more insulated wires, plus a bare ground wire, enclosed in plastic sheathing. Older NM cable may have no ground wire and cloth rather than plastic sheathing.

Old-work box: See Remodel box.

Outlet: Any point in an electrical system where electricity may be used. Receptacles, fixtures, switches, and hardwired appliances are all outlets.

Overload: A dangerous condition caused when a circuit carries more amperage than it is designed to handle. Overloaded wires overheat. A circuit breaker or fuse protects wires from overheating.

Pigtail: A short length of wire spliced with two or more wires in a box and connected to a terminal so that two or more wires will not be attached to a terminal.

Plug: A male connection at the end of a cord designed to be inserted into a receptacle outlet.

Polarized plug: A plug with its neutral prong wider than the hot prong. It can be inserted into a receptacle outlet in only one way, thereby ensuring against reversing the hot and neutral sides of a circuit.

Raceway: Surface-mounted channels made of plastic or metal through which wires can be run to extend a circuit.

Receptacle: An electrical outlet into which a plug can be inserted.

Recessed can light: A light fixture that contains its own electrical box designed to be installed inside a ceiling so that its trim and perhaps lens is flush with the ceiling surface.

Remodel box: A metal or plastic electrical box that clamps to a wall surface (either plaster or drywall) rather than being fastened to framing. A remodel box must have an internal clamp to hold the cable.

Rigid conduit: Metal conduit that can be bent only with a special tool.

Romex: A common name for nonmetallic cable.

Service entrance: The point where power from the utility enters the house. A service entrance may be underground or it may be at or near the roof.

Service panel: A large electrical box, containing either fuses or circuit breakers. Power from the utility enters the service panel where it is divided up into branch circuits. Also called a panel box or main panel.

Short circuit: A dangerous condition that occurs when a hot wire touches a neutral wire, a ground wire, a metal box that is part of the ground system, or another hot wire.

Splice: To connect together the stripped ends of two or more wires usually by twisting them together and adding a wire nut.

Stripping: Removing insulation from wire or sheathing from cable.

Subpanel: A subsidiary service panel, containing circuit breakers or fuses and supplying a number of branch circuits. A subpanel is itself controlled by the main service panel.

System ground: The method by which an entire electrical system is grounded. Usually a thick wire leading either to one or more rods sunk deep in the earth or to a cold-water pipe.

Three-way switch: A switch used when a light is controlled by two switches.

Through-switch wiring: Also called in-line wiring. A method of wiring a switch, in which power runs to the switch box.

Transformer: A device that reduces voltage usually from 120 volts to between 4 and 24 volts. Doorbells, thermostats, and low-voltage lights all use transformers.

Traveler wires: In a three-way switch setup, the two wires that run from switch to switch. See Common wire.

Underwriter's knot: A special knot used to tie the wires in a lamp socket.

Volt (V): A measure of electrical pressure.

Voltage detector: A tool that senses electrical current even through insulation and sheathing.

Voltage tester: A tool that senses the presence of electrical current when its probes touch bare wire ends. Some voltage testers (often called voltmeters) also tell how many volts are present.

Watt (W): A measure of the amount of power that an electrical device, fixture, or appliance uses. Volts × amps = watts.

Wire nut: A plastic protective cap that screws onto two twisted-together wires to complete a splice.

INDEX

METRIC CONVERSION

U.S. Units to Metric Equivalents			Metric Units to U.S. Equivalents		
To convert from	Multiply by	To get	To convert from	Multiply by	To get
Inches	25.4	Millimeters	Millimeters	0.0394	Inches
Inches	2.54	Centimeters	Centimeters	0.3937	Inches
Feet	30.48	Centimeters	Centimeters	0.0328	Feet
Feet	0.3048	Meters	Meters	3.2808	Feet
Yards	0.9144	Meters	Meters	1.0936	Yards
Square inches	6.4516	Square centimeters	Square centimeters	0.1550	Square inches
Square feet	0.0929	Square meters	Square meters	10.764	Square feet
Square yards	0.8361	Square meters	Square meters	1.1960	Square yards
Acres	0.4047	Hectares	Hectares	2.4711	Acres
Cubic inches	16.387	Cubic centimeters	Cubic centimeters	0.0610	Cubic inches
Cubic feet	0.0283	Cubic meters	Cubic meters	35.315	Cubic feet
Cubic feet	28.316	Liters	Liters	0.0353	Cubic feet
Cubic yards	0.7646	Cubic meters	Cubic meters	1.308	Cubic yards
Cubic yards	764.55	Liters	Liters	0.0013	Cubic yards

To convert from degrees Fahrenheit (F) to degrees Celsius (C), first subtract 32, then multiply by 5⁄9.

To convert from degrees Celsius to degrees Fahrenheit, multiply by 9⁄5, then add 32.